HOW TO
STUDY

HOW TO
STUDY

Paul Oliver

TEACH YOURSELF BOOKS

For UK order queries: please contact Bookpoint Ltd, 39 Milton Park, Abingdon, Oxon OX14 4TD. Telephone: (44) 01235 400414, Fax: (44) 01235 400454. Lines are open from 9.00–6.00, Monday to Saturday, with a 24 hour message answering service. Email address: orders@bookpoint.co.uk

For U.S.A. & Canada order queries: please contact NTC/Contemporary Publishing, 4255 West Touhy Avenue, Lincolnwood, Illinois 60646–1975, U.S.A. Telephone: (847) 679 5500, Fax: (847) 679 2494.

Long renowned as the authoritative source for self-guided learning – with more than 30 million copies sold worldwide – the *Teach Yourself* series includes over 200 titles in the fields of languages, crafts, hobbies, sports, and other leisure activities.

A catalogue record for this title is available from The British Library

Library of Congress Catalog Card Number: On file

First published in UK 1998 by Hodder Headline Plc, 338 Euston Road, London, NW1 3BH.

First published in US 1998 by NTC/Contemporary Publishing, 4255 West Touhy Avenue, Lincolnwood (Chicago), Illinois 60646–1975 U.S.A.

The 'Teach Yourself' name and logo are registered trade marks of Hodder & Stoughton Ltd.

Typeset by Transet Limited, Coventry, England.
Printed in Great Britain for Hodder & Stoughton Educational, a division of Hodder Headline Plc, 338 Euston Road, London NW1 3BH by Cox & Wyman Ltd, Reading, Berkshire.

Impression number   10 9 8 7 6 5 4 3 2 1
Year   2004 2003 2002 2000 1999 1998

CONTENTS

TO THE READER

This book is full of ideas to help you with your studies. I hope it will be useful whether you are on a college or university course, or studying on your own. Whatever your subject or interests it is always useful to have fresh ideas to help plan your work. The book includes comments from students talking about the study methods they use.

Nevertheless no two people study and learn in exactly the same way. Not all of these ideas may suit you. Try them out and find the ones which seem to help. By reflecting on your own learning process, you will become much more effective at studying.

Best wishes with your studies.

Paul Oliver

1 | PREPARING FOR STUDY

Having confidence as a student

The main purpose of this book is to help you achieve what you want to achieve in your studies. You may have decided to take up the study of a subject at home or to enrol on a course at college. You may be returning to study after a long break from academic work. Alternatively you may already be working towards a qualification and want to improve your study skills. Whatever your personal situation, there are two things we can certainly say about studying – it can be very enjoyable and it can be hard work!

We would not expect the mastery of a new subject or the gaining of a qualification to come easily, otherwise we might think it was less of an achievement. There is a sense of struggle involved in study, and most people who look back on a period of academic work acknowledge that at times it was hard and that there were sacrifices to be made. Perhaps that is part of the pleasure which study gives – that feeling of striving to understand something and then achieving your goal.

Any activity in life which involves a degree of effort and difficulty inevitably brings some uncertainties, particularly at the beginning. We tend to ask ourselves questions such as:

- Do I have the ability to do this?
- What happens if I fail?
- Can I fit this into my busy life?
- Will I be as good as everybody else?
- Have I got the resources to do this?
- Do I have the willpower to keep going?

These are understandable and very widespread human feelings, and perhaps we should examine them in the context of studying before we go any further. It is difficult to make progress in any activity, and particularly studying, if you have too many doubts and uncertainties. However, when it comes to questioning our ability to learn, my feeling is that if you want to learn something then assume you are able to learn it!

Every new subject seems daunting at the beginning. When we open a book on statistics we might think that we could never understand the formulae. A new foreign language seems to have impossibly complex verb endings. How will we ever learn those? When we first try to use new computer software it never seems to go right on the screen. However our experience of learning things from a very early age tells us that learning is almost always like this. The main thing is to have a belief in your own ability to learn, no matter how apparently difficult the subject is.

One of the main threats to our confidence as a student is when we compare ourselves to others. If you are sitting in a tutorial at college the people next to you may sound so articulate and well-read! Perhaps they just keep talking and explaining all their ideas without seeming to need any thinking time. If you are in a lecture some people may always have an interesting question to ask. When you are discussing a topic with fellow students there are always those who seem to have understood things the first time. We can always find people who appear to be more intelligent than we are, but this may only be an impression or appearance. The main thing to focus on is what you are learning yourself.

One of the best ways of gaining confidence as a student is to feel that you are making progress. This does not have to be a major step forward all the time; it can just involve learning a new, small piece of information. It is often a great help if you can keep a record of your learning. When you have read a few pages of a textbook note down in a couple of sentences the key points you have learned. You then have a sense of achievement. The reading you did has not disappeared into the general day's activities. You have recorded your own progress. You could keep a notebook specifically for this purpose and call it your learning log. When you check back through it your learning log can give you a sense of confidence about your own progress.

If you are thinking of enrolling on a course at college, you will probably get a course leaflet to read. No matter how careful tutors are to make these user-friendly, leaflets can sometimes make the course seem more formal and daunting than it is in practice. There are also usually entry requirements for courses which can sometimes sound rather rigid.

However, many courses will admit people without the formal entry requirements, as long as they show evidence of the ability to complete the course of study. It is always worthwhile making an appointment to see a course tutor, even if you do not think you have the necessary qualifications. You may have some other qualifications or experience which can be considered, or there may be a preliminary course which can be taken in place of entry qualifications. There is an increasing trend to take into account prior learning for entry to courses, even if that learning may not have taken place in an educational establishment. Such a procedure is known as the Accreditation of Prior Learning (APL).

It is sometimes easy to become preoccupied with the possibility of failure as a student. This can be because we have a tendency to be always looking forward to the end of a course or to when we will gain a qualification. We are perhaps worried that all the investment in time and money should come to nothing because we might fail the course. There are really two important issues here.

The first is that in most educational programmes nowadays, there is usually a provision to retake the assessment. A failure is rarely the end of the road. The second is that by always looking forward in time to the end of a course, it is easy to miss the moment-by-moment enjoyment of study. We can become preoccupied with gaining the final qualification and not get the most out of the learning process. Perhaps the best strategy for not worrying about failure is to concentrate on the present moment and the pleasure gained from studying right now. It may be harder to do this in some contexts than others. It is probably harder to do it if you are studying at home on your own, or by distance learning, because if you are with a group of other students you can get enjoyment from discussing the course subject matter. Nevertheless it is always worth trying to get the most enjoyment out of studying here and now, and letting success at the end of the course take care of itself. If you are enjoying your studying and finding it rewarding, the chances are that you will be successful anyway. When we are thinking of embarking on a course of study, one of our main concerns is often whether we will be able to find the time. This is particularly true of part-time students and those studying at home who have to fit study in between other commitments. When students were asked about the difficulties of studying part-time they nearly always mentioned time as the great problem:

'The main difficulties are having time for study when working most of the time; and only having half a day in class each week.'

'Juggling the time between work, family and study. A feeling of continuous tiredness and fatigue.'

When we first contemplate a new course, difficulties like this may seem so daunting that we do not actually start. This is a great shame really, because very often the problems do resolve themselves at least to some extent. When you read the course publicity from a college or university, the attendance requirements may seem very rigid, but when you actually talk to the course tutor things often do not seem quite as fixed or demanding. There is often more flexibility in practice. Moreover there is a very wide recognition in education now that if we are to become a genuine learning society and encourage lifelong learning, then educational establishments have to offer programmes in a flexible way.

Before deciding that you cannot fit a course of study into your life, it is a good idea to have the confidence to approach the college or university and discuss the matter with a tutor. As a potential student you are a very important person to the tutor, and even if all your difficulties cannot be solved you can at least explore the possibility of different attendance patterns. You might very well find that there are alternatives which could not be included in the standard course literature. Even if one college cannot accommodate your needs, you might hear of another course or establishment which can help.

Resources for study come in all shapes and sizes. They can include a computer, books, notepaper, a quiet place to study, access to a library, friends to discuss ideas with, and your tutors. When you are planning to study, it is easy to think of all the resources which you are lacking and how difficult the process will be. Inevitably a major resource when studying is money. Even here though it is possible to reduce costs by trying to explore alternatives. If you have not got the time or money to visit your college or tutor, a lot can be achieved by regular exchanges of letters. Resources are always more effectively used when they are shared, and on this principle one of the best strategies when studying is to develop a network of contacts among your fellow students. This might be done through a sophisticated system of emails, or by writing letters, or organising group meetings at someone's house. The main thing is to meet and talk with other students; exchange ideas; discuss your subject and share resources. This is one of the great pleasures of the academic life, and many people find that once they become involved in study they rarely want to give up. As one person said:

> 'I can't imagine being out of education as a student long-term; both for career development and personal fulfilment.'

Although many people find that studying takes over their lives and that study in effect becomes their hobby, others are concerned whether they will manage to keep up the momentum to finish a course, particularly if it is a long one. Obviously our enthusiasm for study, like any other activity, does ebb and flow to some extent. We all experience times when we feel we are not making very much progress and we do not seem to get our ideas together. When this happens it can be a good idea to take a break and find another form of activity for a while. We might feel that we need a longer break and actually want to stop studying for a while. There is no harm in this and if you are on a formal college course, your tutor will be quite used to students asking to take a break from their studies. In academic jargon there are even terms such as intercalate or intermit to describe this situation. You can usually formally suspend your studies without any penalty, and then pick them up again later.

It is sometimes the case that financial difficulties arise, and people have difficulty paying course fees. The best thing to do here is to discuss it with your tutor, and plan the best course of action. It may turn out that if there is no other solution, you can take a break in your studies until you save up the fees. This might not be the best thing you would have wished, but at least the work you have done already is not wasted and you know you can return to your studies later.

Education is becoming more and more flexible in its structure, and there is an increasing assumption that people will want to stop and start their studies, as need requires. This is really part of the concept of lifelong learning. You should certainly not worry about the possibility of not completing your course in one go. The main purpose of this section has been to try to convince you that you should not let things stop you studying. Have the confidence to start and keep going. It may be harder for some people than for others, but there are a lot of rewards in the process. Jones and Johnson (1990, Vol. 1, p. 19) contains a very useful section on developing confidence as a student. Let us try to summarise a few commonsense principles.

Summary

- Have confidence in your own ability to learn.
- Do not be preoccupied with comparing your progress to that of others.
- Keep a record of what you learn, and gain confidence from it.
- You do not have to conform to a particular way of studying.
- Develop your own learning strategies.
- Make a start, gain satisfaction from your studies, and let success take care of itself.

Thinking about motivation

Many different factors can motivate us to study. These factors can often be very powerful in driving us on to learn something and to engage in what sometimes involves years of work. They will differ from person to person, but might include some of the following:

- The wish to master a particular subject.
- The desire to obtain a qualification.
- The need to obtain knowledge in order to get a job.

These are very instrumental factors i.e. they are dedicated to the achievement of a particular goal. The only problem with these as motivators is that the achievement of them is often far into the future. This means that you may not have any regular reinforcement of your motivation as you are learning.

If, for example, the initial factor which motivated you was to obtain a diploma in Fine Art, this may motivate you for several months but may not sustain you for the two or three years of the programme. You will need other factors to keep you going. Instrumental factors such as the ones above, are often very effective at starting us off on a project, but we need to keep reminding ourselves of them during our studies. Otherwise we tend to lose sight of the main factor which caused us to start on the project in the first place.

The other thing to bear in mind about instrumental factors is that we may not necessarily achieve all of our goals. For example, we may study a subject in order to be better able to get a new job. However, going for a job interview is a very hit and miss affair. The knowledge and skills which we have are only one factor in deciding whether we get the job. There are many other variables operating.

If we built our motivation solely around the instrumental purpose of getting a job, we may be very disappointed if we do not succeed, and this can have a negative effect upon our studying.

Fortunately there are other motivational factors which come from the actual process of studying. These have an ongoing effect and are much less dependent upon the achievement of specific goals. They include such factors as:

- The pleasure which comes from the actual process of studying.
- The realisation that you are gradually learning something which perhaps you thought would be very difficult or impossible.
- Enjoyment of the company of other students, and of the discussions which you have.
- A feeling that you are moving forward in your life and achieving something.
- A sense of being part of a cultural tradition; of learning from previous writers and being able to pass this knowledge on to others.
- The comments and feedback which you receive from your tutor.

There may be many other factors of this kind which motivate you. Many of these factors are likely to be fairly specific to you, because they reflect your own personality and way of looking at the world. We can think of these as being intrinsic factors because they are largely internal to us and come from our own thought processes.

Sometimes we discover these feelings of enjoyment once we have started studying. We cannot necessarily anticipate them. Nevertheless, they can be very strong motivators and help keep us going through a long period of study much better than the instrumental factors such as a desire to get a job.

The great thing about intrinsic motivators is that they are independent of results. We are not striving towards a goal, desperately trying to achieve something. Rather we are just enjoying the process of studying; enjoying the process of interaction with other students. This act of living in the present moment, of simply enjoying what we are doing now, often brings a much greater sense of satisfaction than always working towards something which is in the future.

Feedback, the last factor mentioned in the previous list, is one of the most important motivators. Most learners benefit from a knowledge of results while they are studying. Fortunately the possibility of getting feedback on progress has been helped by the widespread adoption of credit accumulation systems. Most courses are now to some extent, divided up into credits, modules or units. These are accumulated bit by bit, until you obtain the required number for the course or qualification. Tutors can supply feedback on the assessment for a particular module, and also a printout showing the amount of credit received so far on the programme.

When asked about the importance of feedback on their work, students said:

'Feedback is important to me and my learning.'

'It is important to have both written and verbal comments on your work. You can sometimes forget verbal comments after a while, but you can re-read written ones.'

'Feedback helps give you confidence on how to improve yourself.'

'Feedback is very important as it gives you an indication of how you are getting on.'

Apart from stressing the usefulness of feedback, the second quotation above stresses the value of going back to constructive feedback to remind yourself of useful advice.

Summary

- Instrumental motivators can be very useful in encouraging us to start studying.
- Intrinsic motivators are much better in helping us to sustain our interest.

■ Intrinsic motivators are much more about the process of studying rather than the product.

■ Obtaining feedback on your work can have a positive motivational effect.

Enjoying study

You are probably studying either to achieve a particular end, or for an intrinsic, personal reason, or for a combination of both. Whatever your reason, however, it is almost certain that you will be more successful if you enjoy what you are doing. You will probably:

■ Remember facts more easily.

■ Find that you can study for longer periods without getting tired.

■ Analyse assignments more effectively and be more efficient at writing them.

■ Have a more positive attitude to your studies.

■ Develop better personal relationships both with other students and your tutors.

The important question though, is, can you cultivate a frame of mind in which you enjoy your studies, or do you just have to accept whatever mood you are in? My argument is that even if you find yourself feeling despondent about your studies, you do not need to continue feeling like that. You can cultivate a more positive approach which will enable you both to be more successful and also to enjoy what you are doing.

The reason is that most feelings of dissatisfaction about studying are caused by treating it as a means to an end. We want to pass our accountancy exams in order to get a pay increase. We want to pass our Diploma in Management in order to apply for a promotion. We want to speak Spanish fluently in order to speak properly to shop assistants and waiters when on holiday. However, the main problem with treating studying purely as a means to an end, is that all kinds of unanticipated events may prevent our achieving the desired goal.

The accountancy company may cancel all pay increases for staff because of falling profits. The management student may be unable to apply for a promotion, simply because there are no promoted posts available. The Spanish holiday may be cancelled because of an airline strike. Events like this can undermine all the enjoyment obtained from studying. The alternative strategy is not to regard studying as a means to an end, but as something of worth and value in itself. Let us take one or two examples which use this strategy.

Suppose you are learning some dates and the names of events in history. The events might be such things as the accession of a new ruler, a new act of parliament, or a major battle. These kinds of facts can sometimes be very difficult to remember, particularly if you are trying to recall them just for an examination or test. However, try to think of the significance of the event for ordinary people, either for those alive at the time, or for those alive today whose lives have been affected by the consequences of that historical event. For example, in the case of a battle, try to think of such things as:

- ■ What must it have been like on the morning of the battle? What would the soldiers have had for breakfast? What was the weather like? What was the battle scene like? Where had the soldiers come from?

- ■ Were the soldiers regular soldiers or conscripts? Had they written home to their parents, girlfriends and wives? Which regiments were represented at the battle? Which towns and villages did the soldiers come from?

- ■ What weapons were they fighting with? What kinds of wounds were typically inflicted? What kind of medication or treatment was available? What was the survival rate for soldiers who were wounded?

- ■ What happened to soldiers after the battle? Did they go on to fight in future battles? Did they return home? Did the battle resolve any of the initial political or economic causes of the conflict?

You may not have anywhere near all of this information about the battle, and so may not be able to answer the above questions. You may even wonder why you should be advised to think of some of these questions when all you want to do is to remember the name and date of a battle. However, the questions given above are just examples of the kind of question you might ask yourself. They all relate to the fundamental question of what it was like for ordinary human beings to be involved in the battle. Instead of merely thinking of the date of the battle as a fact to be learned, try to think of it as an event shaped and enacted by people just like yourself.

At the start of the battle, as they waited for the fighting to start, some men would have been exhilarated, others frightened, others would have been thinking of their children at home. Try to think of these people as real human beings, rather than cardboard figures from a history textbook. You may then find that it is not only more interesting to study the battle and its consequences, but also easier to remember the date and facts of the battle. Study has become more enjoyable. This technique can be applied to any area of study, and it basically involves always asking yourself about the implications and relevance of what you are studying, for ordinary people.

If you are studying law and must learn a new piece of legislation, it may all seem rather dry and uninteresting. However, try to think of someone who might be affected by the legislation. Try to imagine someone whose life could be drastically improved by this law. Imagine their life history, the things which have happened in their life, and the way in which this law may enable them to achieve social justice. The legislation may then become real, more enjoyable to study and easier to learn. If you can manage to find the relevance for other human beings in what you study, then you may enjoy your studying much more. It will then become studying for a purpose. It will not be, however, a self-oriented purpose, but an other-oriented purpose. You will be studying to help yourself understand the world of others. You can call this approach to studying the Real People Approach. It emphasises study as a process in which you search for the relevance for other human beings.

As a final example let us take the situation referred to earlier, of learning a foreign language such as Spanish. Learning a new language can be extremely tedious, particularly if all you see in the grammar book are lists of irregular verbs and new sentence constructions. Looked at in this way, the learning of a language can scarcely be described as enjoyable.

However, using the Real People Approach, we may begin to see the grammatical constructions as part of a living language; a means of communication between parents and their children; between patients and their doctor; and between friends, young and old. We may well think of these same grammatical constructions used at that very moment on radio and television, and in newspapers and magazines. When using the Real People Approach, try to concentrate particularly on the usefulness and value for achieving good in the world, of whatever you are learning. This is not a technique which is to be taken on faith; rather it is only of value if it really works. Try it with your own studies. It may make your studying more enjoyable and enable you to learn things more effectively.

Summary

- Try not to treat study simply as a means to an end.
- When studying something, try to think of the relevance of the information for other human beings.

Selecting ways to learn

Learning is a very complex activity and it is difficult to prescribe methods which will be guaranteed to suit everyone. The things which we have to learn are not uniform and they fall into different categories. Firstly, we have to learn pieces of information, concepts, ideas and what are perhaps misleadingly called facts. These might be chemical formulae, ways of solving mathematical equations, the names of grammatical constructions, or the functions of parts of the body.

Secondly, we need to learn practical skills. In science this might involve learning how to connect up an electrical measuring instrument or how to analyse the components of a chemical mixture. In geography, it might involve testing the acidity of different types of soil.

Thirdly, when we are engaged in studying, we sometimes learn new values or attitudes about issues. For example as a result of studying crime statistics we might alter our attitude towards capital punishment. As a result of studying aspects of ecology, we might change our attitude towards environmental issues. Studying a subject is not merely about learning new facts, it is also about interacting with the information as a human being, and sometimes acquiring a new perspective on that information.

We can therefore identify three types of material which we learn when studying – new ideas, new practical skills and new personal value positions. It is too much to expect that everyone will learn these in the same way. Some people will learn new ideas simply by being told about them. Others may need to repeat them over and over again before being able to learn them. It also seems reasonable to suppose that practical skills will be acquired in a different way from mental or cognitive skills.

Imagine trying to teach someone to serve at tennis only by describing all of the techniques but not letting him or her hold a tennis racquet or actually practise. You might describe in great detail the techniques for a top-spin serve or a slice serve, but no matter how detailed the instructions, you would not in reality expect someone to learn this without practice.

Now, quite apart from the different categories of information which we must learn, different people clearly possess different abilities when it comes to learning and studying. One person has a natural ear for music, while another will describe herself as tone deaf. One person seems to be a natural player of ball games, while another cannot hit a ball to save his life. One person seems to be naturally good at performing calculations, while another finds anything to do with numbers very difficult. We all have inherited abilities which appear to help us to do things naturally, but besides this there are environmental factors such as our life experiences or the extent to which we work hard at something. A child whose parents own a shop or business is brought up surrounded by ideas like buying and selling, wholesale and retail, profit and loss, and perhaps will find it relatively easy to build upon this background in the fields of business and commerce. The child of parents who own a garage will grow up surrounded by mechanical concepts and skills, and may acquire quite naturally a great deal of knowledge about vehicles. They may or may not have a natural aptitude for business or mechanical things, but they will inevitably acquire some knowledge and skills simply through being in those environments.

From this discussion then, what can we say about learning strategies? The first thing is that because everyone brings a different range of inherited abilities and a different range of environmental experience, we cannot expect people to all learn in the same way. Some people for example prefer to study for short periods of time, and have a change of activity in between. Some students commented on this as follows:

> 'I try to make sure that when I study at home or in the library, that I study often for short periods of time. I like to have plenty of breaks.'
>
> 'I work for a period of about one to two hours, stop, and take time out to do something else, walk, have a chat etc. and then I go back to the books.'

On the other hand there are people who prefer to start working on an assignment and simply keep going until the assignment is finished. A student with this approach commented:

> 'I have storm sessions of intense concentration for a number of hours until the task is done.'

It is evident that people use very different techniques when it comes to learning and that to some extent these do work. The danger is, however, that we adopt a particular method for perhaps the wrong reason – say, because someone else uses it. The best approach is to be reflective about our own learning style. We need to observe ourselves using different approaches, and to try to analyse which method seems to produce the best results. One strategy, for example, is to experiment with different periods of study, and with different periods of rest time between them. This should help you to develop a work pattern which is suited to yourself.

It is also important to recognise that learning or revising for an examination, say, may not require the same study techniques as writing an assignment. For example, it may be difficult to sustain periods of concentrated reading for much more than about half an hour at a time, while you may be able to continue writing or typing for much longer than that.

As a general principle you may find it more productive to combine reading with a practical activity such as making notes, producing summaries on cards or large sheets of paper, or dictating notes into a tape recorder. The regular change of activity can improve concentration and is worth trying out.

Perhaps at this point it is worth making a few comments about the distinction between theory and practice when it comes to learning styles. Theory and practice are not as different as one might think. When researchers investigate different approaches to learning they usually try to summarise their results in broad general statements which become known as theory. Although these ideas are very valuable, it does not mean that they can automatically be applied to everyone. For example, some research might be carried out with a sample of respondents consisting of 18-year-old college students. It does not necessarily follow that the learning approaches they use are the best ones for more mature learners.

It is perhaps most sensible to treat all theory and advice as potentially useful but to experiment with it yourself. Try the techniques which you think may work for you.

Summary

- Learning involves acquiring a wide range of knowledge and skills. We may not all want to use the same learning strategies.

■ Trying to combine theoretical and practical activities is often a useful way to enhance learning.

■ Experiment with learning strategies and find the ones which work best for you.

Choosing the right course

Some people study on their own or in informal groups, but most are probably involved in some kind of organised course. However, you may not be enrolled in a large institution such as a college or university. You may be at an Adult Education class organised by a local authority, or at a privately-run organisation. Whatever course you have in mind, however, there are several basic issues which apply wherever you intend studying:

■ Entry qualifications or experience.

■ Exit qualification of the course.

■ Course fees.

■ Length of course.

■ Resources and equipment needed.

■ Delivery of the course. (Is it part-time or full-time? Are there residential requirements? How long are classes?)

■ Location of the course.

■ Library and computing facilities available.

■ Tutorial support available.

■ Lecturers and tutors on the course.

Nowadays when you are thinking of choosing a course, remember that educational organisations are often financially independent and must raise their own income in much the same way as a business. This means that they have considerable freedom over ways of organising their courses and in determining the fees which they charge. Once you have decided on the type of course you want, i.e. the subject and approximate level, then it is sensible to compare local institutions to see what they have to offer. You could use the checklist and the following discussion to compare what different colleges have to offer.

You will of course already have an idea of the subject matter of your proposed course. You will know that you want a course in ceramics, or accountancy or environmental studies. However, within each subject area there may be a range of courses available, described variously as certificates, diplomas or degrees, and you may not be sure which course to apply for. One way of reaching a decision is to look at the entry requirements. These may vary from no requirements to fairly high-level qualifications. The entry requirement for a Masters degree may be a relevant honours degree or equivalent.

The use of the word equivalent signals an important feature of entry qualifications which is that you should not regard them as absolutely fixed and rigid. There is nothing to stop you telephoning the course tutor and asking for an appointment to discuss the course. Most course leaflets cannot list all of the possible permutations of entry qualifications for a course. All they can do is to state the normal or most common mode of entry and leave the rest up to negotiation with the course tutor. The normal requirement is, however, a guide to the usual standard required for admission.

Entry requirements are usually expressed as qualifications, but this is not always the case. For example, a practical course such as pottery, may be for absolute beginners, or it may assume that you have a basic awareness of throwing a pot on a wheel. The course leaflet will usually explain the skill level which is assumed for entrants.

The fundamental purpose of entry requirements is to ensure as far as possible that all entrants will be able to complete the course successfully. The course tutor will not want anyone to be unable to cope with the early part of the course and thus fall behind. However, you may feel that even though you do not possess the stated entry qualification, you have sufficient experience or simply knowledge obtained through wide reading, to embark on the course. If you consider this to be the case, you should certainly ask the course tutor.

Where such knowledge is accepted as equivalent, it is known formally as the Accreditation of Prior Experiential Learning (APEL) or the Recognition of Prior Learning (RPL). Most colleges and universities have systems for this. You may need to take a short test to demonstrate your knowledge, or you may be asked to prepare a portfolio of evidence to show the kind of work you have done in the past. Equally, you may feel that you possess qualifications which although not the stated entry requirement, are in fact equivalent to it. If this is the case you should again discuss this with the course tutor. Apart from entry requirements you also need to know the final qualification (if any) to be obtained on completing a course. This may be very important to you particularly if you need it to start a career. One important aspect of all qualifications is the accrediting agency. This is the name of the organisation which guarantees the quality and standard of the qualification. For example, universities accredit (validate) their own degrees and are responsible for the standards of those awards. It is common, however, for another institution such as a college, to teach all or part of a university degree. In this case the university still guarantees the standards, but the college is responsible for organising the teaching. The validating body for an award is important because it is the guarantee of academic standards.

The name of an award is also important as in some cases this can be ambiguous. The term Diploma may be used to describe an award for a rather brief and lower level course of study, or for a major course at postgraduate level (i.e. after first degree level). You do need to ascertain the actual academic level of a qualification before embarking on a course. Nowadays with the widespread use of credit accumulation systems, there is an increasing rationalisation of the levels of awards, but it is worthwhile being absolutely clear about how the level of your proposed course equates to that of other courses.

For anyone considering a course of post-compulsory education, fees are a very important issue. It is essential to recognise that the fees for a particular course may not be the same at two different institutions, even if they are located near to each other. It is important that you compare institutions and fees. Course costs can differ quite substantially.

Moreover, some courses make extra demands upon students, such as requiring them to buy textbooks or even computers. It is important to check up on the resources provided by the college or university, and those which they expect you to provide. There can sometimes be substantial extra costs here. Again, policies may vary from college to college. The same qualification may also differ in the length of time taken to obtain it. An obvious example is that of three- and four-year degree courses. Some degree courses include an extra year for an industrial placement or for a year abroad, and yet the same degree qualification is obtained at the end. The extra year can involve substantial extra costs. If you consider an extra year or a longer course, it is important to be clear about the purpose and to ask yourself whether you need that experience.

It is also worth clarifying how much of the extra time you have to organise yourself, and how much is organised by the university. You need to know whether the university is responsible for organising an industrial placement. If so, it is worth asking about the details of this. Which companies have been used in the past? How many placements have led to employment? Does the university organise accommodation if the placement is away from your home? Practices may vary widely from institution to institution. It is worth finding out the details of the situation. Very often the same course is offered on both a full-time and part-time basis. You will need to find out details as it may affect your other commitments. The term full-time may not prove to be very accurate, particularly with regard to the total number of hours of lectures or classes. The description full-time relates to the assumption that for the length of the course, the institution considers that a student needs to be studying in one form or another for most of the week (and not holding a full-time job). Annual tuition fees for full-time courses are often substantially higher than for the same course offered on a part-time basis.

In terms of course delivery you will need to ask for details of the length of course classes and whether there is any regular tutorial support. You may not be able to get to all of the regular classes and it may be important to have access to a tutor at other times. However, one-to-one tutorials are very expensive for institutions to provide. It is much cheaper to have a tutor teaching a group of fifteen or twenty students simultaneously. Nevertheless, it can be important for your progress to have occasional access to your tutor on an individual basis and it is worth asking about this.

Before finally committing yourself to a course you may want to ask the names of the tutors; to find out the location of the classes; and perhaps to look at the library and other facilities. You may know some of the tutors teaching on the course, and want to ask if you can have a particular person as your tutor. Colleges and universities sometimes have annexes and premises spread widely apart. You want to be sure that the course is being offered at a location which is easily accessible to you. Finally you may be studying a minority subject and want to reassure yourself that there are books and other facilities to support your learning.

You may think that there are a lot of things here to ask about, but the atmosphere of education has changed a great deal in recent times. Education has moved much more to being a commercial enterprise which markets courses as a product, and with the student acting as a consumer.

The result is that as a student paying course fees you are purchasing a product and you want to be sure you are getting what you want. Some aspects of the product may vary from college to college and from university to university. Ask around and compare prices. Make sure you are getting what you want. If not, try somewhere else.

Summary

- Make sure the course will give you the qualification you want.
- If you do not have the standard entry requirement, discuss this with the course tutor.
- Think about any previous learning you have achieved, and whether this might be relevant.
- Compare course fees at different institutions.
- Remember that you are paying the fees (directly or indirectly) – make sure you enrol for the course you want.

Being a part-time student

One of the first things to realise is that if you are a part-time student, then you are in the majority. Most Further and Higher Education students are studying part-time; and this does not count all those people who are studying informally and are not enrolled on a college course. While both full- and part-time students have many educational needs in common, there are still some potential areas which can pose difficulties for part-time students.

Let us start with an obvious but important area – access to resources. College and university libraries are open during normal working hours, but part-time students often have difficulties getting there during these times. Most institutions do their best to resolve this issue by opening in the evenings and to some extent at weekends. However, education is very expensive to provide and there is never-ending competition for resources within institutions. The result is usually a compromise in opening hours which probably does not meet everyone's needs.

Another aspect of academic library provision is the concept of 'short-term loan'. Books which are very popular or in demand because they are recommended course texts are sometimes only loaned for twenty-four hours at a time. If they are not returned on time, there are often heavy fines. The short-term loan may be even shorter with books being only allowed on loan for a few hours. Such systems can be very difficult for part-time students. A full-time student can borrow a book, consult it, make a few notes, and then return it on time. The part-time student may be dashing in to the library and then have to leave to meet some other commitment be it work or family.

The main thing to remember here is that systems are human creations, and they can be 'un-created'! However, the people who create them may be operating with the very best of intentions, and simply may not be aware of the difficulties and problems created by their systems. So try telling them, in the nicest possible and politest way. You could perhaps write a short letter explaining your personal difficulties. Admittedly, you are only one student, and as far as you know everyone else may be happy with the system. However, if you can point to the general ill-effects of the system and show that it is likely to adversely affect other students, then you may be able to get it changed. At the very least you will have explained your situation and that may make you feel a bit better.

Part-time students frequently say they have difficulties using a library. The following comments from students seem like cries from the heart:

> 'I never have the relevant books at home when needed.'
>
> 'The book problem is one I cannot overcome as I always seem to have the wrong book with me.'
>
> 'My big difficulty is only having irregular access to university facilities like IT, library and staff.'

It is generally going to be more difficult for part-time students to take advantage of library facilities. Full-time students can call in at the library several times in the day to check if books are available, whereas this is always more of a problem for part-time students. Nevertheless there are aspects of the typical library system which can be used to advantage. The reservation system can be very useful, and libraries usually write to you when a book is available for collection. Also if you have a circle of friends or network of fellow students, you can arrange to pass books on to each other when you have finished with them. You can also perhaps take advantage of the journal collection. Normally journals cannot be borrowed and you have to photocopy the articles you want. This facility does not favour either full-time or part-time students, and journals usually provide much more up-to-date material than books.

Some of this may sound as if the prospects as a part-time student are fairly bleak, but fortunately many people feel quite the opposite. There would not be so many part-time students if it was not rewarding and if it was not possible to make progress towards success. When asked about the rewards of studying part-time, here are some of the things which people said:

> 'I like the flexibility – it allows other aspects of your life to continue, especially work.'
>
> 'The flexibility is good, although a constraint is lack of time to study.'
>
> 'There is a feeling of achievement against the odds and a raising of self-esteem.'
>
> 'I prefer still being able to earn a salary – feeling more fulfilled and confident.'
>
> 'I feel I am achieving something for myself, and not relying on a supervisor to recommend promotion.'

One of the main themes emerging from these quotations is a feeling that part-time study enables us to carry on with all the other important aspects of our lives. We can continue our jobs and careers if necessary, and this can help to avoid the financial pressures of being a full-time student. Tuition fees are also usually much less for part-time as opposed to full-time students, and in addition the completion period for courses is not necessarily much longer.

Nevertheless there are aspects of part-time study to which you can give attention, and which will perhaps help your performance. The very fact that you are keeping other aspects of your life going, means that you have to manage your time very carefully. We look in detail at some strategies for helping you with organising your time in Chapter 4, but it is worth noting here the importance of this when you are a part-time student.

You should not be put off the idea of study simply because you cannot imagine how you can fit it in. There will obviously be times when you have to work hard even when you are tired, but there are all sorts of small savings in time which can be made, and these redirected towards your studies. It is often not difficult to reapportion our time, as long as we are motivated to do so, and gain a lot of satisfaction from what we are doing. It is not too difficult to give up watching a television programme if we are getting a sense of satisfaction from the reading we are doing. Many people speak of the psychological and practical benefits that they receive from studying. When asked about the reasons for wanting to study part-time they replied:

'To achieve something special.'

'To obtain awards.'

'To increase my personal bargaining power in the commercial world.'

'I did not get an opportunity earlier on and I want to change career.'

'For re-training purposes.'

If you are a part-time student you will probably have found that it can be difficult getting to know other students. If you are a full-time student you will have plenty of time to go for a coffee after a lecture and discuss things. You can get to know other students socially and also have time to discuss assignments and the work which you are doing at the moment. There is a great deal of incidental learning which goes on during such informal meetings, and we should not underestimate the importance of peer learning and support.

Such interaction is much more difficult for you as a part-time student. You may have to dash into college, go straight to your class, and then rush away afterwards. You may get to know one or two people in class, but it can be quite difficult. You can thus feel quite isolated and cut off from contact with other students. There can be practical disadvantages for you in terms of learning:

■ You might be having difficulties understanding a topic and think that you are the only one who does so. In fact, perhaps everyone is having the same problem.

- Perhaps you are having a problem printing something off on a computer. Other people will probably be helping each other with tips and hints, which you do not have access to.

- Learning by discussing and exchanging ideas is one of the main ways in which we learn. Having to explain an idea to someone else is one of the best ways of understanding it yourself! If you do not have anyone to talk to, then you are not having the benefits of this kind of learning.

- There can be a strong sense of psychological isolation in these situations. One of the great pleasures of being a student is to feel that you are part of a community of learners who are all moving in the same direction and have the same kind of interests.

It is possible to do something about these drawbacks but you have to work hard at it. Basically you have to create the kinds of networks which tend to exist naturally for full-time students. There are lots of things you can do to make contact with others.

One of the best is to offer help. If you hear of a student who is having difficulty getting a book or an article which you have, then offer to lend it. If you realise someone is having a problem with computing, and you think you know a solution, offer to show it to them. If you know of a place to buy inexpensive stationery, then share the information with others. Helping people is a mysterious thing. Once you start offering help to others, it does not seem to take too long before they are helping you with something. Before long you have got a real learning network going.

Next best to offering help, is to ask for help. If you are having difficulty finding a book in the library, ask another student if they have found it. If you are having problems with a particular piece of software ask someone to assist you. You will soon start to share your learning with others.

There are lots of simple things you can organise in class to help develop a sense of community among part-time students. Ask your tutor to announce a get-together one evening. Alternatively, suggest circulating a piece of paper for everyone to write down their names, addresses and phone numbers. This can then be photocopied for all those who contributed to it. You could build in agreed ground rules about not phoning each other at particular times. Alternatively, individuals could attach notes of when they would prefer not to be phoned.

Another idea is to suggest that those students who are interested write a paragraph about themselves and their own particular academic interests. These are then combined into a newsletter and photocopied and circulated among contributors. This enables students to identify others who have similar interests and to communicate with them.

It may be necessary for you as a group to agree certain rules about the circulation of such information, notably perhaps that it will only be circulated to contributors. However, this should not pose too many problems, and the potential benefits are enormous in terms of bringing people together who have similar academic interests.

Even if you are at present studying at home on your own and not enrolled on a formal course, there are all sorts of opportunities for meeting people with similar academic interests. The use of electronic communication such as email and the internet has opened up enormous possibilities if you have the right computer facilities; but more traditional options like clubs and societies are still important. The main thing is that unless you especially want to, learning and studying on your own is not necessarily the best, most enjoyable and most effective way of going about things. There is enormous fun and benefit to be had from joining the appropriate community of students.

A related issue for part-time students is communication with tutors. If you are a part-time student and have tried ringing your tutor at college or university, you know it can be very difficult to make contact. Tutors are out of their rooms for a good part of the day. They may be teaching, attending course team meetings, in the library, or at exam boards to mention only a few of the varied academic activities in which they engage. This, however, may not be very reassuring to you, if you have just phoned four or five times without success.

Full-time students have the benefit of often coming across their tutors around college, and stopping for a quick chat to discuss a topic. Part-time students unfortunately miss out on all of this informal and incidental interaction. Also, as part-time students have many other commitments, it may not always be possible to keep to arrangements for tutorials. This only compounds the problem. The only solution is to set up very carefully-planned communication systems with your tutors. Here are some ideas.

First of all, produce a piece of paper or card with all of the relevant information about how your tutors can contact you. Include on it some or all of the following information:

- Your full name.
- Home address and telephone number.
- Work address and telephone number.
- A summary of the most convenient times for your tutor to telephone you.
- Any dates you are on holiday.
- The course and modules you are studying.
- Commitments which might prevent your attending classes/ tutorials at any particular time.

Carry plenty of photocopies of this around with you and give one to all of your tutors. You might be able to produce a reduced size version as a kind of business card to hand out. Another alternative is to purchase a roll of pre-printed, self-adhesive address labels. Again, you can give these to your fellow students and to your tutors. That deals with communication from your tutor to you, but what about the other way round.

Make a chart on a piece of paper with the names of all your tutors down the left-hand side. When you meet them, collect a few basic pieces of information and add these to your chart. You may need to know some or all of the following:

- Tutor's name.
- Address and room number.
- Telephone number including extension number.
- Fax number and email address.
- Days and times in the week when your tutor is likely to be available to receive telephone calls.
- Any days when your tutor is frequently away from college or university.

If you set up these communication systems at the beginning of your course then you should be able to minimise communication difficulties.

Another important thing to check with your tutor is the procedure for submitting coursework. Some organisations have postboxes for assignments; others ask you to send work to an administrative office from which you receive a receipt. As a part-time student it may be awkward for you to call in to deliver an assignment to a postbox, and if this is so then you need to make careful arrangements with your tutor for posting work.

If you are on a course where a lot of the teaching is done by one-to-one tutorials then you may find it helpful to explore different ways of communicating with your tutor. It may not always be convenient for you to come in to college to meet staff. One way is to agree with your tutor that you will post drafts of part or all of your assignment work, and for your tutor to send back comments. Another strategy is to have pre-arranged telephone conversations. It is surprising how much discussion can take place in a ten minute phone call. The advantage is that the conversation is often very focused. Both you and your tutor are aware of the relatively short time of the conversation and make a special effort to stick to the main points of the subject. You may find that such discussions are much more efficient in terms of time than face-to-face meetings, and in addition you save the travelling time.

This has been a quick look at some of the factors and issues affecting you as a part-time student. Other matters such as time management will be dealt with in different sections of the book. The main thing, however, is not to see part-time study as in some way second-best to being a full-time student; but rather it should be viewed as a window of opportunity which can redirect and reshape your life. McGivney (1996, p. 65) contains some interesting data on part-time study.

Let us try to review a few suggestions about part-time study:

Summary

- Share resources with other students.
- Help to create networks of students.
- Offer help and ask for help.
- Learn by discussing and debating.
- Set up systems for communicating with tutors and students.
- See part-time study as a window of opportunity.
- Tell others about your academic interests.

Returning to learn

In a sense the term return to learn is something of a misnomer because we learn throughout life in a variety of ways. However, it has come to mean the situation where someone who has had a long break from formal study, decides to take up an academic course somewhat later in life. Sometimes people in this category have not studied since leaving school.

It is unfortunate that some people when they were at school found the experience less than rewarding, and this can result in a lack of interest in academic learning. Nevertheless many find that later in life something sparks off an interest or perhaps they need to take up study to help them with getting a job. There is a growing realisation that academic learning will need to be a part of many people's lives on a continuous basis. Students commented on this as follows:

> 'The changes in technology and the peaks and troughs of boom and bust economies, mean that people will need to be able to adapt. This will only become possible through lifelong learning.'
>
> 'As a mature student who has also undergone professional training, continuing to learn has the advantage of expanding the breadth and depth of my knowledge, and this has value for me in all areas of my life.'
>
> 'I cannot imagine being away from education long term, because it is so important to me for career development and personal fulfilment.'

These arguments seem very sensible, but they may not help you if you are feeling uncertain about your ability to return to learn. Some people have no difficulty in getting back to academic work, but others may have uncertainties in some of the following areas. You may have a feeling that education has moved on since you have been away, and that you do not have the skills to cope with modern systems of learning. There may be a particular fear with regard to computing skills. There may be a fear of failure which is related to doubts about ability to complete a course. There may be a concern about mixing with younger students and seeming to be the odd one out. In addition, memories of school days may make it difficult for people to feel comfortable in a large college or university. One person once explained to me about how nervous they felt when approaching the large, imposing entrance to a college.

All of these feelings are quite natural, but if you are in this position at all, you should focus more on what you can bring to a course and to a college. You can contribute so much.

Yes, you may have to learn some new skills, but that can be rewarding. However, think of all the practical experience of life you have gained while away from study. Academic learning is not just about theory, it is also about applying theory to practical situations. You may find yourself far better able to do this because of your extra life experience. You may also be concerned about possible failure, but this is much less relevant in our modern educational system. The approach tends to be supporting students to succeed, rather than trying to identify those who are not good enough.

You will probably find a wider age range in the college you attend, than you expected. Most people find that studying with people of a variety of ages can be a very rewarding experience. People have different things to contribute at the different stages of their lives. Finally, if a college or a university seems rather imposing or off-putting, remember that the university is not the building. The real university consists of the people who work there, and their main function in life is to provide a service and help you, the student.

If you are thinking of going back to academic study, there are probably one or two useful strategies you could consider adopting. These may help you start to develop some of the skills which you need and may save you time when you start the actual course.

Many colleges offer a variety of access courses, return to study courses, or taster courses which are designed for those going back to study. They may last from a few days to a term in length, and can be very useful in helping you to readjust to an academic environment. You will meet other people in the same position as yourself, and practice such skills as assignment writing and looking up references in a library. Alternatively colleges and universities often operate an associate student scheme whereby for a small fee you can have access to all of the computing, library and other resources. This does not purchase time on a course, but in practice you may also be able to receive advice from technician and support staff on computing skills for example. You would need to make enquiries at your local college about what the fee covers.

In other words, there are ways of starting to readjust to academic study without taking the plunge of enrolling on a full-time course. The main thing is to take the decision to start, even if you take it slowly at the beginning.

Summary

- When you return to learn, you take a lot of valuable life experience with you.
- Make enquiries about short access courses which may help with updating your skills.
- Consider becoming an associate student and developing your computing and library skills.

Being a mature student

There is not a precise definition of a mature student, but he or she is probably aged over 25 years, working full-time or part-time to support themselves and perhaps dependents, and with the range of commitments that we tend to accumulate as we get older. This may not be a completely accurate picture, but the image we have is of someone with a very busy and complex life. Trying to fit in study as well, inevitably adds to that complexity. This is how some students described their lives:

'The time it takes to complete a degree programme seems to go on for ever. It is very difficult to concentrate and to remove your mind from other things when studying. Reading time is very necessary, but it is difficult to allocate it and stick to it. Having to use family time to study is always a difficult decision.'

'I try to cope with a full-time job, a part-time job, and family commitments, and this means that time is a very precious commodity and must be used wisely. I sometimes feel guilty taking time out for leisure activities. Time management skills are very important and a supportive family essential. Some things have to go on hold.'

'I work full-time and also attend night-school in the evenings. It is always difficult to complete all of the modules, as well as making sure I have a home-life.'

Anyone who has tried to combine study with employment and family life, will recognise themselves in these extracts. Sometimes things do have to simply go on hold. It is often not possible, even with the best will in the world, to keep up with all your previous commitments. If you decide to give priority to your studies, then something else may need to be set on one side.

One useful strategy is to make sure you explain to other family members the kind of studying you are doing. Your spouse may understand anyway, but if you have children they may not understand fully why mum or dad disappears for hours at a time, or complains because the television is too loud. You could try showing your children the work you are doing and comparing it to their schoolwork and homework. You could show them an assignment you have written, and the mark and comments you received.

You will probably find that they are very interested, and there may well be connections between what you are studying and what they are learning at school. This can lead to some interesting discussions which can be very useful for children. It is also a good opportunity to explain to them about further and higher education, and that they may well find that like you, they will need to think about continuing their education throughout life.

There is sometimes a sense of guilt about studying when you feel you could be spending time with the family. Probably the best strategy is to share your studying with family members rather than keeping it as something simply for yourself. Treat your study as a genuine family activity. Tell them about the things you are learning; initiate discussions; mention books you are reading; tell them about your lectures; and if possible, relate your studies to current events around the world, and topics which appear on the television news. In this way your studies contribute to family life rather than existing separately from it.

You will probably find that the amount of time you spend on your studies fluctuates week by week and month by month. You may have regular attendance requirements at college, and the amount of time you need may depend on when you have to hand in assignments. A good idea might be to prepare a calendar or a wall chart showing in bright colours the times when you will need to do more studying. Family members can refer to this and know when mum or dad is likely to be busier.

However, study is an open-ended activity. You can go on and on for ever, and there are always new articles to read and further notes to take. It is always best to have a cut-off point in mind, and tell the family that you are finishing at 7.30, and then the whole family is going to the cinema! That way you will probably use your time more effectively and your family will know when they can start talking to you again. It is important for them to be able to plan their time as well. Besides that, definite points of relaxation are important for you too, and will improve the quality of your study time.

Summary

- Discuss your studies with other family members.
- Prepare a calendar of your study timetable so that others will know when you are busy.
- Put a time-limit on your study.

2 IDENTIFYING YOUR LEARNING RESOURCES

Making your own resource pack

When you are a student you may find yourself studying almost anywhere – at home, in your flat, at college, in a library, on a bus, or perhaps when just waiting for someone. It is very useful if you can carry all of the essentials for studying with you, in a compact, portable form, so that you can work wherever you find yourself and maximise the use of time.

Some students nowadays carry all kinds of electronic and computing equipment with them. It is not unusual for students to take out laptop or palmtop computers to take notes on during lectures; nor is it unheard of for students to leave lectures to receive a call on their mobile phone. Digital cameras are used to capture images and integrate these with text on a computer. Electronic personal organisers for keeping a record of tutorial times and lectures are also used. While all these can be immensely useful, you do not need to invest much money to have a very effective resource pack to support your studying. It is not so much the money invested, but the idea which is important.

Let us start with a few very basic but useful items. A pocket diary is almost essential for noting key dates such as irregular tutorials, examinations, key lectures, hand-in dates for assignments and such things as conferences to be attended. Such a diary can be very small and inexpensive, and simply used to record dates.

You could also try keeping another type of diary which is more comprehensive and perhaps more accurately called a learning log. This is a record of your learning and can be recorded in a variety of ways. You can write an account day by day, of all the things you have gleaned from your reading, or reflections on your lectures. Alternatively you could divide it up into subject sections and keep notes on your observations about what you are studying. Such a log serves two purposes. It is a valuable record for you to read and revise some of the things you have learned, and also the actual process of reflection is valuable in itself. Reflection and writing helps you to analyse ideas and filter them through your own consciousness. For your learning log you could try using a journalist's pad or a small, hardback notebook. These are easily portable and convenient to use.

An address book is an extremely valuable aid. You can use it to record phone numbers and addresses of both other students and your tutors. Do not forget as well that fax numbers and email numbers are very useful, if you can find them out. It is also worth keeping a note of names and addresses of authors and academics. You may get the addresses of people at academic conferences for example. Also, at the end of articles in academic journals, you will often find the address of the author. This is to enable readers to correspond with the author if necessary, about issues raised in the article. It may be worth keeping a record of names and addresses and of the area of research associated with each person.

Equally, most academic journals have a book reviews editor who is happy to receive reviews of recent, relevant books whether or not these have been supplied by the journal. Writing and publishing book reviews is a very useful way of getting into print, and it is a good idea to keep a record of the names and addresses of review editors, and of the journals with which they are associated.

Certain types of documentary information are useful to keep in your resource pack. If you are enrolled at a college or university you may have a student identification card which may also be used for borrowing from the library. You may have been allocated a login number in order to access the computer system. A photocopy card may also enable you to pre-pay for a certain number of copies. Keep all of these readily accessible.

You will need a pad for taking notes in lectures, and a variety of stationery items will come in useful. These might include a few envelopes, plastic wallets, overhead projector transparencies and pens, stamps and a white eraser pen for correcting typing errors. A roll of self-adhesive name and address labels for yourself can also be very useful in lots of ways, from naming your possessions to quickly producing a self-addressed envelope. A spare computer disc is very useful. You can easily make protective pockets for discs by cutting up pieces of plastic bubble paper the appropriate size and sealing them around three edges with sellotape.

Among stationery items, a luminous highlighter pen is very helpful for noting sections on photocopies of journal articles which you regard as especially significant. These are also useful for highlighting sections of your own notes when you are revising.

Finally, if you have a regular weekly study timetable of lectures, meetings and tutorials, then it may be helpful to prepare a small timetable card which summarises your commitments, and lists the names of tutors and rooms and times of lectures. The purpose of your resource pack is to create all the essential items for a portable study, so that you can maximise your use of time, and study effectively wherever you happen to be.

Summary

- Try keeping a learning log of your reflections on your studies.
- An address book of colleagues in your academic network is very useful.
- Keep a record of names and addresses of authors and book reviews editors from academic journals.

Collecting useful books

One of the most important resources when studying is your own collection of books. It need not be expensive to acquire a small reference collection, but an important decision involves which books to purchase for regular use and which to acquire through an academic library.

A rough and ready distinction can be made between general reference books, and specialist, subject-based works. Normally it is best to borrow the latter from a library. They can be fairly expensive and may need to be ordered from an academic bookshop. However you may well come across useful specialist works in a second-hand bookshop, but care must be taken that anything you choose is not too dated in its approach or information.

Whatever subject you are studying, there are a few categories of reference books which you will find useful. Perhaps the most obvious example is a good dictionary. Of obvious use to a student of English language or literature, a dictionary can be helpful in any subject. There is probably no subject area where at some stage you do not need to express yourself clearly in your own language. Subjects such as history, sociology and religious studies demand essay-writing skills with a clear need for a good dictionary. In science subjects however, you need to write clear and accurate laboratory reports, and in geography for example, you may need to write up an account of field studies investigations. Although mathematical symbols are used to express ideas in science and engineering, language is an essential medium for such functions as expressing hypotheses, arguing logically and analysing concepts. It is always good practice to extend your vocabulary, and to select alternative and perhaps more precise words. Dictionaries can help in this process, but a thesaurus is specifically designed to aid the location of synonyms and related words. A thesaurus is a classification of words which provides alternatives and words which are of similar meaning to the key word of the subsection. Generally a thesaurus is not concerned with technical or specialist words, but with those which are of general use.

A dictionary of quotations can be a very useful reference work to have. Such dictionaries contain quotations from a wide range of well-known people which are relevant to a broad range of disciplines. For example, there will typically be quotations from scientists, musicians, artists, actors, writers and politicians.

Apart from their general interest, quotations are very useful for introducing essays or for including in academic writing for illustrative purposes. Some quotations are very witty or express complex and subtle ideas in a few well-chosen words. For example, some authors use a quotation at the beginning of a chapter to set the tone for that section or to encompass the broad theme.

Subject dictionaries such as, say, a Dictionary of Astronomy or a Dictionary of Sociology are very useful in your subject specialism. However, it is important to remember that a dictionary and the terms selected for definition are not absolutes, but reflect the particular perspective of the compiler. Not all dictionaries of a particular subject will select the same terms to define. Most of the central concepts of the subject should be present, but there will almost certainly be many differences. Dictionaries can also become dated fairly quickly, particularly in a rapidly-evolving subject. Imagine the relevance of a Dictionary of Information Technology which was compiled a decade ago. Dictionaries of scientific subjects can become somewhat dated as a result of advances in knowledge.

There are some dictionaries available which bring together terms from a variety of subjects. A good example is *The Fontana Dictionary of Modern Thought* (Bullock and Stallybrass, 1977) which combines terms from mathematics, religion, technology, and the social and natural sciences among other areas. This can be a very useful type of reference work because it enables you to make connections between terms in different disciplines. At times, a good one-volume encyclopaedia can serve the same purpose.

All of us from time to time are unsure about a point of grammar, or whether we have expressed ourselves correctly. This is where a copy of a book of English usage comes in very useful. There are a variety of versions available, and these help enormously with matters of expression where it is often difficult to locate the answer in a dictionary.

Finally, for those of you who are doing some fairly formal academic writing such as a dissertation or long project, a Style Manual can be very helpful. This provides guidance on the standard ways of referencing, using quotations, abbreviations and acronyms. It also provides advice on the layout of theses, reports and research articles. Some universities produce their own guidance notes on these issues, whereas there are books which combine style notes with advice on academic writing. Examples of some of these types of reference works can be found in the bibliography at the end of this book.

Summary

The following types of general reference books are very useful as learning resources:

- An English-language dictionary.
- A thesaurus.
- A dictionary of quotations.
- A subject-specialist dictionary.
- A single-volume encyclopaedia.
- A guide to English usage.
- An academic style manual.

Making notes

The taking of notes is such a common activity for students that it is perhaps surprising that strategies for note-taking are not discussed more often. The first aspect of notes is that one does not necessarily take them for the same purpose or under the same circumstances.

For example, if you are taking notes prior to writing a long essay, you may wish to make fairly detailed notes. On the other hand, if you are making notes to act as a revision sheet for an exam, you may only want to write down a few key headings to remind you. Equally, there is a world of difference between taking notes at speed and under pressure in a lecture, and making notes at your leisure from a textbook. The assumption of this section is that both the purpose and the circumstances of note-taking affect the strategy you should adopt. Most of the discussion will concentrate on the taking of notes in lectures, as this is a fairly difficult and complex task. At the end of the section, there will be a discussion of note-taking for one or two specialist purposes.

Note-taking in lectures fulfils several different functions:

- As an aid to understanding the subject matter.
- To summarise the subject matter.
- To provide a record for revision purposes.
- To provide a summary to help with writing coursework and assignments.
- As an aid to concentration during the lecture.
- To identify the key concepts.

As in most aspects of study skills, different students adopt different procedures. There are those who basically try to write down as much as possible. Here are quotations from students who fall into this category:

'I like to write very full notes, as for me it helps focus my mind on the lecture material. I have on occasion used a recorder.'

'I try to write down everything and then consult with others to establish any omissions.'

'I use speed-writing. I have trained myself to be able to write virtually everything a lecturer says.'

'My aim is to write as much as possible with clear unambiguous headings.'

'I just jot down notes, not in any kind of format. At times my handwriting can be unreadable. I make certain that I copy down information from the overhead projector and whiteboard.'

Clearly there are people who feel that trying to write down everything is a useful strategy. However, there are several reasons why this may not be the best approach. Firstly, lecturers often introduce all kinds of peripheral comments, and digress at times, during the lecture. They may do this to add interest to the topic or for illustrative purposes. These comments are usually not part of the central information and not worth committing to note form.

Secondly, if you write down everything which is said your notes are going to be so long, it will not be very easy to re-read them or to revise from them. In any case, unless you are able to use a form of shorthand, then it is likely that they will be almost illegible. A third problem is that you will be so busy actually taking notes that you will be unable to reflect very much upon what is being said. You will not have the time to formulate questions for example, or to think of possible arguments against what the lecturer is saying. You will be reduced to a writing machine rather than a person who is using the lecture as a vehicle for learning.

Nevertheless, there are some very useful suggestions in these quotations and these are noted below with some comments:

- Use of a tape-recorder. This can be helpful, but it is a courtesy to ask the lecturer's permission. However, the result will be a collection of tapes which will need a lot of time to play through. The purpose of note-taking is to reduce the quantity of information you have to cope with.
- Note-taking is a useful aid to concentration in a lecture and can help you to think about what is being said.
- Discussing the lecture with others afterwards. This is often done by students anyway; but it is a good idea in helping you to fill gaps in your understanding.
- Using headings in your notes. This is very helpful as it enables you to subdivide information into manageable

topics. Notes with subheadings are generally easier to read, understand and revise from.

■ Copying from the overhead projector and whiteboard. Lecturers often use the overhead projector transparencies to prepare the key points of a lecture and hence to act as a prompt for them. By making sure at least, that you note down these points, you can be certain that you have a record of some key material from the lecture.

Although some students try to write down everything in a lecture, others restrict themselves to a few key points. This is much more in the spirit of what we tend to understand by taking notes. However, there are a number of associated strategies which people use. Here are some examples of what students say:

'When taking notes in lectures I tend to use bullet points and incomplete sentences in order to summarise what is being said.'

'I try to note down the key points and write extensions when I am particularly interested in something or feel it is relevant.'

'I try to write down the main topic titles and to identify the nouns.'

'My main strategy is to abbreviate words. I have become very used to listening to the tutor at the same time as writing.'

'I put down the core word and then if I have time, I write a quick explanation of it. If I don't have time, then at least I have the core word.'

'I write down the key terms or phrases, and then read up on them after the lecture.'

This strategy appears very sensible but it does beg the question of how we identify the key points in a lecture. The lecturer may help by telling you – perhaps by using a transparency which highlights the main points. On the other hand, you may use your own judgement, and depending upon the content of the lecture, you may pick out those concepts which either seem central to the argument, or else you feel will be very helpful in enabling you to recollect the content of the lecture.

The first quotation above talks about the use of bullet points. These sometimes tend to imply a sequential ordering of the material. Certainly the use of numbers implies an order of some sort. Some lecturers do try to present their material in this format, and this helps the student in preparing sequential notes. It must also be admitted that some material, perhaps mathematical or scientific information, or aspects of grammar in a language, do lend themselves particularly to a logical, sequential delivery and presentation.

However, in other subjects or in other contexts, sequential presentation of the lecture and sequential note-taking, may not be the most appropriate form. For example, in the analysis of the meaning of a poem, all kinds of ideas may be generated in your mind almost simultaneously. These ideas may be interwoven and difficult to present in a particular order. We will return to this issue later when we discuss the work of Tony Buzan.

Two students suggest the strategy of writing down key words followed by a brief commentary if they have the time. This represents something of a compromise between very brief notes and trying to write down everything. One student suggests reading up on key concepts after the lecture. This is probably a very useful strategy if you have the time, as it will reinforce what has been said in the lecture.

Another main strategy used by students is that of adding substantially to the notes after the lecture, by rewriting and expansion where necessary. Here are some quotations from students concerning this approach:

> 'I scribble down the key facts and often rewrite the notes, preferably as soon as possible after the lecture.'
>
> 'I extract the main points in rough, and then re-copy following the lecture.'
>
> 'I try to take down the key points as notes, and expand upon them later.'
>
> 'I take the relevant points down and expand on them when I write them up.'

If this approach is combined with careful listening and reflection during the lecture, then it can be a very effective means of learning. The act of adding to the notes necessitates thinking back over the lecture and reflecting on the subject matter. Although a very helpful approach, this system is also very time-consuming.

One student emphasised very clearly the importance of reflecting on the material taught:

> 'I try to arrange the ideas in my own mind. The most efficient notes are those that have been thought about and written in my own words rather than those of the lecturer.'

When you are doing this, try to reflect on what the lecturer is saying, and think of ways in which this might affect the lives of real people. Note down some of the ways in which real people might be affected.

Finally, several students advocated a rather different approach to note-taking, that of making notes in the form of maps or flow diagrams. It was suggested earlier that not all information may be best summarised in linear form or sequentially. Here is what two students commented:

> 'I try to use pattern maps usually, or just key points and headings.'
>
> 'I use my own shortening of words; and also flow diagrams and arrows.'

As a society we do tend to use information which is presented in a linear, sequential form. We express ideas in numbered order, or chronological order, or order of importance to us. It can be argued that this is merely a convention – although perhaps a very useful convention. Tony Buzan in his very well-known book *Use Your Head* (1989) has particularly drawn our attention to this, and in order to reflect this aspect of the brain's activity, he recommends the presentation of notes as Mind Maps® – a diagram showing the connections between ideas. To illustrate the approach, let us take an everyday rather than academic example, and imagine that you are making enquiries at a travel agent about a trip abroad. You want to know as much as possible about the country, travel procedures, currency and local customs. You make notes as the discussion proceeds. In effect, the travel agent is your tutor and you are the student.

If you made conventional linear notes they might look like this:

1 Passport – check it is not out of date, and get visa form on plane.
2 Currency – get small denominations.
3 Travellers' cheques/credit cards.
4 Lockable suitcase.
5 Check tetanus injection.
6 Travel documents – collect one week before travel.
7 Get taxi from airport.
8 Make sure to use hotel safe.
9 Hire car prices seem expensive.
10 Wood carvings are best souvenir – be prepared to haggle.

A Mind Map® of the same conversation could however, look something like Figure 2.1.

There are perhaps several difficulties with the numbered notes. Firstly, they are written down in the order they occurred in the conversation and this may not necessarily be the order in which you wish to plan your travel arrangements. Secondly, notes inevitably involve the use of unnecessary linking words, which are not central to the issue. Thirdly, the ideas are not grouped in any way, but simply listed. In the case of the Mind Map® however, it is possible to develop the key ideas from the central picture, and then to extend each key idea into as many strands as are necessary. Superfluous words are omitted and only the key words are noted.

These then are some ways of taking notes. There are many strategies available and it is probably best to pick an approach which meets the circumstances in which you find yourself. Mind Maps®, for example, may prove very effective in lectures, because you can isolate the key concepts and still have the time to do a good deal of listening and reflection. On the other hand, if you are making notes from books and journals for an essay, you may wish to write much more. Perhaps the best advice is to think carefully about the advantages and disadvantages of each approach and to do a little experimenting.

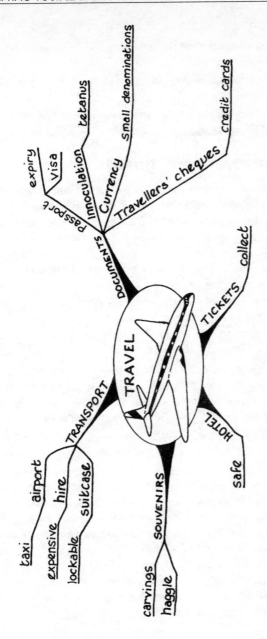

Figure 2.1 Example of a Mind Map® showing a conversation with a travel agent

Summary

- The type of notes you take may depend on your purpose and on the study context.
- Try to restructure material in your own words when you take notes.
- Linear notes may not be the most appropriate style for you.
- Try using the Mind Map® approach of Tony Buzan.

Making a reference guide

Effective studying is a matter of not only having the correct information but knowing how to access it in a very short time. A good example is the type of problem that can arise when you are checking your references in an essay or other assignment. It is easy to include a quotation in an early draft of an assignment, and only make a note of a few of the bibliographic details. You may make a note of the book title and the author's surname and that is all. You realise as you prepare the final typescript that you need the author's initials, the year of publication and the page number from which you took the extract. At the very least you are now going to have to go and find the book in the library. This may not be too much of an inconvenience, providing you remember which library you used.

You may be using, say, the public library and two academic libraries. Unfortunately you may need to invest a little time to locate the original details. Even when you get to the library, unless you can remember the exact location on the shelves, you will need to go back to the catalogue to find the class number of the book.

It is so much better if you keep a reference guide containing information such as this. The guide can be kept on a computer disc or in a simple hardback notebook. Whatever the medium, the strategy is the same. For every book which you either refer to or quote from, keep a note of the author and title, the class number from the book spine and the library from which you borrowed it. This will enable you to trace it easily in the future. Meanwhile, try to make a note of all the correct bibliographic information the first time you use a quotation, but in case you forget, then you have the required information to help locate it again. In your reference guide you can divide books into sections depending upon author, subject matter, publisher or by any other criterion which is helpful to you.

There are many other types of information which are very useful to record in your reference guide. CD-ROMs are an extremely valuable source of information, and when you find one which might be of use in the future note down its name and location. Some discs hold summary information on newspaper and journal articles, including abstracts of articles.

There are also discs which have the full text of articles, and these can be searched by subject, author or according to other criteria. There are also large-scale books such as dictionaries and encyclopaedias which are transposed on to disc so that the text can be made available through the computer. The range of material available through CD-ROMs is enormous and includes, for example, Hansard and government statistical data including records of the latest census.

As a student you will find very useful information on both television and radio. There are many programmes on current affairs which in effect, become serious historical data; and also authoritative talks on all kinds of subjects. You can make notes on these and catalogue them in topic areas.

For those using the Internet, the accessing of information can be greatly speeded up if you know the exact location of data. Each site on the World Wide Web, for example, is identified by its own specific Universal Resource Locator (URL), the by now familiar combination of letters and abbreviations separated by dots or oblique lines. Knowing the URL enables you to go immediately to the information you require. As you become familiar with the more useful Web sites for your studies then it is a good idea to record and classify their URLs in your reference guide.

Your guide can also include information on courses of study which you might follow in the future. It is now becoming the norm for all colleges and universities to have their own Web sites on which they record information about all current courses, enrolment procedures, entry requirements and final qualifications. There is also often information about course content and the lecture programme. The general trend towards higher education becoming more consumer-led is resulting in universities providing more and more marketing information.

There are many important and useful pieces of information which you can include in your reference guide. If you keep it methodically and update it regularly, it will become an essential supplement to your studies. Here are some additional ideas for things to include:

- The names of leading academics and their institutions in your specialist area of study.
- The names of leading writers.
- The names of specialist libraries, museums and art galleries.
- The names and addresses of specialist book shops.
- The titles and a summary of well-known research studies in your area.

Summary

- Keep a record of name and location of both books and CD-ROMs.
- Classify all the URLs which you have found useful in locating Web sites.
- Keep notes on colleges and universities and the courses which they are offering.

Building up a reference collection

Even though you may use libraries a great deal, it can also be very useful to build up your own reference collection or archive. We all have access to a wide range of information, much of it inexpensive. It simply needs storing, collating and cataloguing.

Newspapers are an obvious source of data, especially for certain subjects. You may be able to persuade friends who subscribe to different serious newspapers to pass them on to you. All you need then is the time to sift through them and cut out the articles of relevance. They can be pasted on stiff paper and kept in lever arch or box files. If you don't have a filing cabinet at home, collect narrow cardboard boxes from supermarkets, cut them at an angle and stand them side by side on a shelf. They are excellent for keeping files, magazines and cuttings in classified order.

When you collect cuttings and photographs make a note of the date, page number and name of the newspaper in case you ever wish to quote from it in an assignment. Journal articles are another useful addition to your reference collection. Again, note all the important bibliographic information.

Sometimes academic libraries discard back copies or duplicate copies of academic journals, and it is worth asking library staff if they are considering this, to let you know in advance. Similarly, surplus or under-used textbooks may be discarded, or perhaps sold off very cheaply. You may be able to add to your reference collection in this way.

Data which you have collected yourself is also very valuable and should be catalogued as part of your collection. The data may be numerical or it may consist of interview transcripts. Friends may also give you copies of data which they have collected, although before you use it you should ensure that the respondents gave their permission for such use. You will also need to acknowledge the source of the data, and explain when using it, that it is secondary data.

There are a number of inexpensive, small and portable audio tape-recorders on the market and these can provide a very good record of all kinds of useful events. You may (subject to copyright and/or permission) tape-record lectures, discussions and tutorials. All of these can be very helpful for research and assignments, and are worth collecting and cataloguing. You can also reference them if you need a quotation, by stating the date, context and individuals present.

The nature of educational courses is changing and there is an increasing emphasis upon your ability to collate information and to show the relationships between different types of knowledge. In the past there has tended to be a greater emphasis upon learning a particular body of knowledge and upon relying on the lecturer to give you a specific list of books to read. The lecturer would typically define very carefully the things you were expected to learn and what you would be tested on.

Although there are still syllabuses and lists of learning outcomes (aims) for courses, lecturers expect you to be able to show that you can find information for yourself and integrate pieces of information into an argument of your own. This is where a reference collection is a great help. If you have a range of materials available, then it is much easier to demonstrate these skills when you write assignments. In addition, there are great savings in time and energy, because your reference materials are readily to hand.

Summary

- Collect cuttings of articles and catalogue them by subject.
- Collect copies of reference materials, journal articles and data.
- Practise the skill of making connections between writers, articles and theories, and looking for things which they have in common.

Using computer printouts

Computer-based learning and in particular the use of the Internet and email, have already revolutionised studying and education, and clearly more innovations will come year by year. If you are enrolled as a student at a large college or university then you will have access to such facilities and be able to use their potential. However, if you are studying on your own at home and not at an institution, then if you can afford computer facilities and a printer, you will experience the full potential of computer-based learning. Although you certainly do not need a computer to study effectively at home, let us assume for the moment that you have one and discuss the potential for your studies.

One of the major advantages is that with an Internet connection you no longer have as much need of a conventional academic library. You have access to databases of publications, and even more exciting, to virtual trips either to museums, art galleries, or abroad. Some of these facilities are also available on CD-ROMs. A virtual visit to an art gallery is much less exhausting than the real thing, and you do not need to walk through apparently endless interconnecting rooms to get to the specific paintings or collection you want. You can select what you want to see, and spend all your time studying it. No one could suggest that the virtual version is the same as the original, but getting to see the original may be so impracticable, that the computer version is the only alternative.

Increasingly you can find on the Internet resources which it is simply impossible to gain access to. Museums are now producing virtual versions of medieval manuscripts and of archaeological treasures which, for fear of damage, are simply unavailable to the public. This is an enormous advance in the availability of information, and brings the treasures of the past right into your living room via the computer.

If you need to search for journal articles, this has been made much easier by the indexes of academic journals which are available via your computer. World Wide Web sites provide details of articles which have been published in previous issues of a journal. Some journals are now published via the Web as computer-based journals.

The wide availability of this diversity of information means that the skills of studying are gradually changing. Skills of absorbing and memorising large amounts of information are much less necessary when information is so freely available. On the other hand, when you are faced with large amounts of information, it is important to be able to understand the basic concepts and to be able to make connections between them in order to gain an overview of the subject field.

One strategy for doing this is to print those pages which interest you particularly and then highlight the concepts which seem to occur most frequently. Then start looking up ideas and concepts in conventional dictionaries and encyclopaedias. Try to begin to understand the way the concept is used, and particularly the way it occurs in different fields of study. For example, French Existentialism can be examined as a School of Philosophy, the inspiration behind certain literary works, or perhaps as a practical psychological approach to life. As you understand the concept more thoroughly, you will appreciate its applicability to different fields such as philosophy, literature and psychology. In a society of wide knowledge availability, it is not knowledge per se which is important, but the capacity to see the relationships between different categories of knowledge, and therefore to be able to put that knowledge to greater use.

Summary

- Use CD-ROMs and the Internet to explore the wide availability of knowledge in your area.
- Explore the range of information about academic journals now stored on different Web sites.
- Collect and catalogue printouts and use a highlighter pen to identify the key concepts.

Developing your networks

One of your most important resources as a student are the networks of which you are a part. Networks can provide you with all kinds of help when you are studying:

- Network members can help you identify learning materials, whether paper or computer-based.
- Network members can combine into learning groups to support each other with, for example, a difficult part of a course.
- Network members can provide useful contacts when you are seeking to change your course into a career.

Simply by virtue of the structure of our lives, we are all part of networks. For example, local neighbours can constitute a network, and also other members of our class at college. However, for the purposes of this section, a network refers to a group of people who are connected through study or employment, who share certain common professional or academic interests, and who make an effort to remain in personal contact in order to offer and receive mutual help and guidance.

Central to the idea of study networks is the notion that peer learning can be just as significant as self-learning or learning from a tutor. Peers understand our problems and difficulties, usually because they have gone through them themselves relatively recently.

Networks do not happen by accident. You need to cultivate them. You may not, for example, find that you make friends with everyone in your tutorial group. The main thing is to identify people who have similar academic interests and a similar approach to their studies. Having done this you need to discuss with them ways in which you can support each other's learning. You will need to exchange addresses and telephone numbers if you both feel that the relationship will help your studies. Email is particularly useful in this sense. When you meet people you can ask them if they would like to be put on your circulation list for certain types of information such as summaries of journal articles you have read. Warn them that others on your circulation list would thereby gain access to their email address. If they are happy about this, then you can add their name to your circulation list.

You may wish to accumulate a number of different circulation lists depending upon the information you are likely to circulate to each. The advantage of email is that information can be sent to a network of people simultaneously and thus with great economy of effort.

As a student you can probably learn from your tutors in respect of networking. University lecturers have for long appreciated the importance of being in contact with colleagues both in their own country and abroad. They try to stay in close contact with colleagues who are interested in the same subject and particularly those who are researching in the same specific area. Members of networks such as this tend to write to each other, exchange emails and meet up at conferences or on other occasions whenever possible. In this way they can exchange information on their current research and where necessary collaborate on projects or perhaps jointly write a journal article. It is very difficult to imagine the academic world functioning adequately without networks of this kind.

There is no reason why you cannot replicate these kinds of networks as a student. There are many opportunities to communicate with other students either in your own or neighbouring institutions. Networking has tended in the past to be restricted to groups of people who could meet in person, but the advent of electronic communication now means that you can remain in effective contact with your peers all over the globe.

It is important to remember that networking is a dynamic activity. You cannot simply regard yourself as being part of a network and leave it at that. You should continually be thinking of ways in which you can help your various networks to evolve and grow. It is important to think of things which you can contribute to your network, such as:

- When you receive an interesting document, think of those who might find it useful and send it to them.
- If you hear of a potentially useful meeting, circulate people about it.
- When you meet people with similar interests, add them to your circulation list.
- Work hard at keeping in contact with people.

The last point is particularly important. Study networks atrophy if the members do not maintain regular contact. There is a need for regular writing, phoning and emailing, and in particular regular face-to-face meetings. Electronic communication now enables us to discuss documents on our computer screens while having a visual image of the person with whom we are communicating. The complexities of human interaction probably mean, however, that there is no real replacement for person-to-person interaction.

Finally an important aspect of study networks is that they can be very helpful in providing job and career opportunities. On a course you may, for example, meet part-time students who are in employment and actually in senior positions in their organisation. These network members may be helpful in letting you know of vacancies or of perhaps giving you an informal reference.

Networks are by their nature somewhat unpredictable. There are often many unanticipated outcomes from network membership. One cannot of course assume that wonderful opportunities will automatically result.

Perhaps the main benefit to result from network membership is the great enjoyment to be had by meeting and getting to know other people, and by finding ways to be of help to others. There will almost certainly be reciprocal advantages, but these will develop spontaneously and emerge naturally from the network of which you are a part.

Summary

- Learning from your peers can be as important as self-learning or learning from your tutors.
- Networks do not happen by accident; they need developing and nurturing.
- It is more important to give than to take from networks.
- Develop circulation lists of peers who are significant for each other for different reasons.

3 STRUCTURING YOUR LEARNING

Finding a place to study

Whatever activity we are involved in, it often seems that we are intrinsically happier and more relaxed in some locations rather than others. Tennis players may feel that they always play better on one court rather than another; golfers may have their favourite course and cricketers their favourite pitch. Whether this is an amalgam of subjectivism, superstition or reality, the fact is that we often feel we do perform better. That is the important thing.

Certainly when it comes to the highly-complex process of studying, it is understandable that we tend to have our own specific requirements when it comes to a place to study. If asked most of us could probably list a series of characteristics of our idealised study location. Whether we manage to achieve all of those is, however, another thing. I suspect most of us never quite manage to achieve our perfect environment and yet still succeed at our studies. What is often required is the ability to achieve some of the essential characteristics while compromising on the rest.

You may feel, for example, that you simply cannot concentrate with a radio or television on in the same room. If that is the case then that becomes the predominant requirement, and everything else is secondary to that. Alternatively, you may need to work in short bursts and keep getting up for a break, a cup of coffee, or a walk outside. This might mean that you need to study in a location where you will not disturb others.

You may be in a position where you live on your own, and to some extent can create your own study environment. Perhaps the only decision to make is whether to study at home or at a college library. Perhaps the real difficulties arise when you are a family member and there are many demands on the living space in your house.

You are lucky if you can set aside a room especially for study, and leave all of your books and materials set out permanently. However, you may not be able to afford this luxury. If not, you probably need to identify several different locations which suit your requirements at different times of the day. You may know, for example, that the family generally vacates the kitchen for the lounge after about 7.30 in the evening. This may give you a couple of hours at the kitchen table before people start appearing to make supper. This is where your own reference pack is very useful. You need not be tied to any one location, but can easily move as the situation demands.

Although most people find a degree of peace and tranquillity necessary for study, there can be a danger in too quiet a location. It is very easy to suffer from concentration lapses because your surroundings are too quiet. You may find that you work particularly slowly, when there is no outside stimulus. Sometimes knowing that you may be interrupted from time to time, gives you a sense of urgency to make progress in the time which you have.

While on the one hand it is possible to strive to create the ideal place to study, there is an alternative way of looking at the issue. That is to always be looking for study opportunities wherever you are, and to be choosing the type of studying appropriate to the location. Reading or learning notes may be perfectly possible on a bus or train, when note-taking would be impossible. Note-taking may be possible, however, in a station waiting room. The main prerequisite for taking advantage of these locations is to have your resource pack with you as often as possible.

Finally, one important aspect of studying can be conducted almost anywhere, even without any physical resources, and that is thinking. There is no rule which says you cannot stand at a bus stop and analyse a concept; or walk through a park thinking of good descriptive phrases to use in your next essay; or commute to work on the train while reflecting upon a sociological problem. Fortunately we carry our brains around with us. The only precaution is not to be reflecting on academic matters when we should be using our brains for important practical matters like driving safely.

Summary

- Find places that suit your own learning style.
- Reflect upon how much stimulus you either need, or can cope with in your learning environment.

■ Learn to adapt the type of study to the location in which you find yourself.

Setting targets

When we are studying most of us set targets for ourselves of one kind or another. The most obvious kind of target is when we enrol on a course and want to gain a particular qualification. We aim to complete the course and gain a new qualification, which we may want in order to start a new career or perhaps simply for the satisfaction of gaining it.

This kind of target has a specific end-point, that of gaining certification for the course. With other kinds of study, the target we set ourselves may be a little more imprecise. We might join an evening language course at our local community college with a view to being able to communicate a little better when we next go on holiday abroad. This is a fairly general target, which might also encompass slightly more precise images. We might imagine ourselves at a street cafe in Barcelona ordering our meal in reasonable Spanish, or being able to stop and ask directions from a passer-by in Paris, or reading a newspaper in French. These targets are important for us, because they can act as very strong motivators while we are studying. We may book our holiday in Spain, and then carry around with us the image of our ordering food in Spanish. This image will often keep us working hard at our Spanish grammar when otherwise we might have begun to lose interest.

These kinds of targets are very important but fairly long-term. We know that we are not going to achieve them overnight, but they very often can sustain us during periods of reduced interest in our studies. When we bring these targets into our mind then we are reminded of the original reasons for starting on our course of study.

Short-term targets are also very important when studying. We may decide that we want to complete an assignment one week before the official submission date. We may decide that we want to learn how to insert page-breaks into our text when word-processing. We may make a special effort to understand the solution to a problem in mathematics.

These kinds of targets are very important because they act as staging posts along the journey of studying. The achievement of each one becomes a significant reward to us. We feel that we have made progress. It is equally important, however, that we should not set short-term targets which are too difficult to attain. In this case we can easily become disenchanted because we do not manage to achieve our targets.

The kinds of targets we have discussed so far can be described as intrinsic targets. They are determined by us because we regard them as significant in some way. However, we are also subject to extrinsic targets which are set by our tutors, or are part of the regulations of the college or the examining body for the course we are doing. Common examples of extrinsic targets are assignment submission dates and examination dates. It is part of the process of studying formally that we must learn to meet extrinsic targets. Generally, it is often easier to do this if we are accustomed to setting and meeting our own intrinsic targets.

Here are some of the things which students say about setting and meeting targets:

'I set myself targets each day – to complete x, y and z by the time I go to bed. I then try to complete certain tasks within time blocks that I have set aside.'

'I make a timetable and create deadlines, and then I keep to them.'

'I set myself a deadline as to when I want to finish my note-taking, and then a deadline for when I want to complete the assignment.'

'I plan what needs to be done and organise it into a priority order. I have a notebook with all my work that has to be done in it, and when it has to be finished by.'

These students sound extremely well-organised and clearly feel that setting targets is a helpful strategy. It is important to remember, however, that targets are created to help you and not to hinder you. When you set yourself a personal target, remember that you have done it as an aide and not to make yourself a slave to the target. If it proves unrealistic to achieve then do not be disheartened, but revise the target and have another go.

All kinds of things get in the way of our achieving study targets. When we have a clear evening and are just about to settle down to a good session of work – a friend calls and invites us for a drink; relatives drop around for a chat; the children just will not settle down to sleep; or the phone never stops going. The best laid plans ...

The patterns of life are never predictable, and certainly never seem to be with regard to study times. One thing to learn from this is to set yourself intrinsic targets which give you some leeway for preparing assignments. Try to set targets which will ensure the assignment gets finished a few days before the submission date. Then if something unanticipated happens you should complete it on time.

All of this may sound very organised and rational. Nevertheless I have met people who always seem to have a last minute rush close to the deadline. It is almost as if they need this sense of urgency to motivate them to complete the assignment. Well, everyone is different when it comes to studying, and we need to organise ourselves and create the kind of targets which help us work. The main thing is to reflect on the process of setting targets and plan your work to suit you.

Targets can be very useful as part of the process of planning a long piece of work. A project for example may seem to stretch ahead for a long time, but it can be broken down into a series of reasonable targets. The first target may be to complete a library search on the topic of the project and to compile a list of resources and books. The next target may be to complete a rapid read of these resources. The third target could be to sketch out a draft plan, section by section, for the project. These targets can easily take some of the stress out of a long piece of work, by breaking it down into more manageable units. As you achieve each target you begin to feel that the project is possible after all.

Targets can be conveniently adjusted to suit your own circumstances. If you are particularly busy with other activities, then set very modest targets so that at least you sense you are making some kind of progress. Part-time and mature students often have difficulty feeling that they are making progress with their studies, because of the many other commitments which they have gradually accumulated. If you are in this position then targets can be very useful to give you a sense of achievement. Your target can be as limited as you want to make it. If you are cooking tea and waiting for the potatoes to boil for example, you might set a target of reading just one particular paragraph of a textbook. It may not be very much, but such small increments of study time do build up.

Try making a list of small targets for a day, then a week and then a month. The targets do not need to be very great. Tick them off as you manage to achieve them, and you may be very surprised at what you have managed to do.

Summary

- Targets can be short term or long term; intrinsic or extrinsic.
- They are important to help us structure our work and to motivate us.
- Set targets for yourself which are reasonable and attainable.
- Completing your study targets gives you a sense of achievement.

Reflecting on your work

It is often difficult to complete a piece of work in one go, or to learn something for an examination all at once. Most of us need time to think about what we are doing. We may need to get right away from study and to make no conscious effort to think about our studies, even though from time to time we find ideas coming into our minds. We may need to re-read what we have written and consider whether it makes sense. We may need to think about the theoretical ideas we have put forward and consider whether these seem to apply to practical situations.

This kind of break from systematic work is very important for a number of reasons. It allows us to stand back from our work and see it in more objective terms. When we do that we are more likely to spot errors or to see better ways of expressing our ideas. Especially when we are learning facts or revising for an examination, our minds can become fatigued with the intensity of the work, and we need time to sit back and thoroughly absorb what we have been reading.

In their comments about study techniques several students referred to their need for a periodic break from study:

'When I am planning to write an essay, research and reading come first. I then want a week to ten days to digest the information and sort it in my head. Then I try to sit down and make a passable first draft at the keyboard.'

'I always study by doing an hour's work and then having an hour off.'

> 'When working on an assignment I make notes from as many sources as possible. Then I leave it for a few days – during which time I write down all the ideas which come into my head.'
>
> 'I start by attempting an essay plan, then reading more literature, and then re-evaluating the essay plan.'
>
> 'I think about the assignment over a couple of days, and then plan it.'

These quotations all seem to be pointing to the same need when engaged in studying: that of allowing time for the mind to sort out ideas and put them into some sort of order. This process of reflection often involves the analysis of concepts, and the clarification of our thoughts on an issue. This is a process which often takes time in order to explore the ways in which a concept is used. For example, we might be thinking of the idea of an educated person and exactly what it means to be educated. We might start by assuming that educated is the same as knowledgeable in the sense of someone who wins a television quiz show. We might think of someone with a very wide general knowledge and who is very well-read, and think of them as being educated.

However, as we reflect on the idea, we might perhaps think of someone who is very knowledgeable about a topic but who for various reasons we would not want to term educated. Perhaps the person does not display an apparent moral understanding of the topic. He or she may not appreciate the ethical issues inherent in the knowledge specialism. Alternatively he or she may not appear to be able to see the practical utility of the knowledge possessed. They may not be able to apply it to the lives of ordinary people. They may not possess the ability to test their understanding against everyday experience.

Now the features of a person who we might wish to regard as educated are not necessarily straightforward and easy to delineate. We may need to think very carefully about them, and this process of reflection can take time. As you try to reflect upon your studies, you may well wish to apply them to people you know or have heard of, or perhaps to the lives of imaginary people. Through the process of reflection you will then test your ideas against your experience and have a better idea of their practical value.

Summary

- ■ When reflecting on your studies, try to apply them to the lives of real people.
- ■ Test your ideas against your own experience.
- ■ Try to analyse the concepts which you have used, and explore their application to new situations.

Getting the most from reading

Reading academic literature can be very time-consuming. By its very nature academic writing is often very detailed, making reference to other works in order to support or illustrate arguments, and often based upon extensive data or research. The result is that if you try to read everything which you can find connected with a subject, you will do an almost endless amount of reading and very little else. Then you will have insufficient time to write essays or projects or plan assignments. Reading is obviously one of the most critical aspects of studying, but it is important to manage it efficiently, so that the reading stage does not go on for too long.

The secret of efficient reading is to:

- ■ Learn to be selective in what you read.
- ■ Know when to complete the reading stage of your studies.
- ■ Develop strategies for rapid reading.

It is obvious from student responses that they have developed a number of strategies for selecting reading which they consider important:

'I check the index for the relevant pages relating to the particular topic being investigated.'

'I look for relevant chapters and titles and only read those sections. I glance through that part to see if it is relevant, and if so I read it properly.'

'I skim the introduction and conclusion first and then read in a more focused way if I think the material is of relevance.'

All three of these students show an awareness of the need to be selective in reading academic material. There are many different aspects to this process of selectivity. If you are enrolled on a formal course you will probably find that you will be issued with a course or module reading list. This might be termed a list of references or a bibliography. Such a reading list might consist of only a few general texts or it might be a very detailed list of books, journal articles and other references.

When tutors supply detailed lists of references for a course it is not necessarily intended that you should read every work on the list. The main purpose of providing such lists is as a compendium of references to give you an idea of the general literature associated with a topic. It helps to map out the field of a particular subject and also give you an idea of the most significant writers associated with a subject. Also, you should not necessarily regard such a list as being in any way complete. It is probably intended by the tutor to be indicative of the broad area of the subject.

Another way in which you may receive a reading list is as pre-course reading. When you are accepted on a course you may be sent a brief list of introductory works for you to consider reading prior to the actual start of the course. It is usually not considered essential for you to read these as you will probably have had to meet various entry requirements for the course anyway. They are generally offered for you to keep in touch with the subject matter during a holiday, or to widen your knowledge slightly before starting on the formal studying for the course. It is often not regarded as essential to read all books on a pre-course reading list, but perhaps to select one or two which seem particularly interesting.

Unless you are in the position of being a full-time researcher and able to immerse yourself in the literature of a fairly narrow field, you will need to be highly selective in the books and articles which you read. In order to be able to identify the articles you want to read, it is necessary to develop filtering strategies to identify the ones to read, the ones to consider reading if time permits and those which you will not attempt to read. Fortunately, books and articles provide all kinds of clues about their contents and you can interpret these prior to making a decision.

In the case of academic articles the first and most obvious clue is the type of journal in which it is published. Journals will specialise not only in the subject matter of the article, but also, for example, in terms of the type of research methodology which has been used. You can also read the abstract at the beginning of each article. The abstract is usually of between 100 and 200 words and is printed in italics at the beginning of the article, just after the title. The abstract provides a summary of the whole article, including the general scope and subject matter, the research methodology, the kind of data collected and the nature of the conclusions. By reading the abstract you can make a reasonable judgement as to whether the article will be sufficiently useful or relevant for you to read.

Much the same principle applies with books. The summary on the back or inside front cover will usually provide the essence of the contents, while the Introduction should provide a little more detail. Try to decide whether the book seems relevant to your needs.

Another very useful strategy with both books and journal articles is to consult the bibliographies and lists of references at the end. When you do this you quickly begin to recognise certain names cropping up again and again. It will not be long before you get to know the key books in an area but also the most significant writers. If you then come across another work by one of these writers you may then decide to read it purely on the strength of the frequency with which the writer is cited in other books. Through this process you begin to map the literature of a subject area and to appreciate how different writers are connected with each other, and the particular type of contribution they have made to that field.

When trying to identify an article to read, or to explore the range of the work of a particular author, we are helped considerably by the collections of abstracts of articles which are available on CD-ROM. You can, for example, identify a key word, and then explore the articles which include such a key word in their abstract. This kind of cross-referenced database of abstracts makes the process of mapping a subject literature not only quicker and easier, but more rational and systematic.

In some subjects you may find you have a choice between reading a work by an original author or well-known theorist who first enunciated the key ideas, or of reading a text which is essentially an interpretation and attempted explanation of those key ideas. Which should you read? There is no easy answer to this question, but one or two suggestions may be helpful. It is always very interesting to read the original work of a famous author or thinker. There is a sense in which you feel you are receiving the ideas straight from the mind of their originator. However, if the writer was working some years ago, then what was written was very much part of a historical context. The advantage of a book by a commentator or later academic is that the ideas can be described within that historical context, and very often the ideas can be summarised in a much shorter space than that used by the original writer. The danger, however, is that by the time later academics have added their own ideas, there can be a tendency towards greater and greater complexity.

Sometimes you may come across anthologies of short, but pertinent, extracts from the work of greater thinkers on a particular subject. With this kind of book you almost get the best of both worlds. The extracts are usually selected because they are particularly significant. You have the advantage of reading the original, but in pieces of manageable length.

One aspect of being selective is to choose the articles or books which you will read, but the second stage is to decide which parts you will concentrate on. Some academic books may be 400 or 500 pages in length. It is unrealistic to try to read all of them. Here are two comments by students about how they go about selecting parts of books to read:

> 'I skim-read the whole of a textbook and try to jot down the gist of what the book is saying. Then I re-read in more detail the parts which are important.'
>
> 'I tend to scan the book first and then pick out areas where the key words I am looking for are to be found. Then I read these sections again.'

Both of these students have obviously developed the art of scanning a page to see whether it is significant. This is a useful technique to try to develop. Of course, you can also gain clues from looking at the contents page or index of a book. You should then be able to identify the sections which seem to be of particular relevance to your subject.

Reading is probably the central activity of studying and academic work, and it is important to work hard at developing effective and efficient ways of absorbing information. Otherwise, reading can become extremely time-consuming and interfere with the other main activities of studying such as writing and discussing ideas with other people.

Summary

- You will only be able to read a small fraction of the material on a subject.

■ Selectivity is therefore very important.

■ Develop strategies to identify the books and articles you will read, and which parts of those works you will give most attention.

■ Practice scan-reading and noting the key words and terms only. This will speed up your reading.

Coping with attendance requirements

Most courses in Further and Higher Education specify specific times when classes will be held and also state the number of classes throughout the academic year. Many students find no difficulty in attending the required classes, but for some people, particularly part-time students, there can be real problems. Classes may clash with work commitments or they may fall at times when parents must collect children from school. Even if classes are held in the evenings or weekends, there can still be many difficulties in terms of looking after children or making arrangements for child-minders. If you have difficulties in satisfying all of the attendance requirements for a course, it is best to discuss this with the course tutor at an early stage, and it is often possible to make alternative arrangements.

Attendance requirements for a course are the result of a number of factors, and it may be worthwhile to discuss some of these briefly. When institutions are planning courses, they have to decide on the total attendance to be asked of a student, whether full-time or part-time. This is likely to be determined by a combination of two sorts of factors – economic and academic.

On the one hand, the institution must decide approximately how many hours of teaching it can provide from its various sources of income, such as fees or grants. On the other hand, there are decisions to be made about how many hours of tuition a typical student should need in order to make adequate progress on a course. People may differ in their opinions on both of these questions. For example, when a validation panel approves an institution to offer a particular course, it may make recommendations about the total teaching time. Sometimes external or professional bodies may have an opinion on this, and certainly tutors teaching on the course will have found from experience how much time they consider is needed to deliver the course. In short, the total teaching hours for a programme are not absolute, but derive from a range of considerations.

Quite apart from the total hours for attendance on a course, there is the issue of the timing of classes. This is affected by several factors including, for example, when tutors are free from other teaching commitments. In addition, however, institutions do try to fix classes at times which they believe will be convenient to their potential students. To do otherwise would be rather self-defeating as clearly colleges and universities need students just as much as students need to enrol on courses.

This last point is important because of the nature of the student–institution relationship. Nowadays it is very much a client – or customer–provider relationship. The college produces a product – the course – and the student purchases that product if it is considered suitable and reasonably-priced. The student obviously has an obligation to try to meet the course attendance requirements, but the institution must also offer the course at times and under circumstances which are attractive and convenient to the students.

If you do not think you will be able to attend all of the course sessions, you should certainly not feel embarrassed about negotiating attendance requirements with your tutor. This is a very common practice and it should be possible to reach a reasonable compromise where you attend sufficient sessions to make progress on the course.

There are particular circumstances where you may need to inform others. If your fees are paid by a local authority or by an employer, then they will probably assume that you are attending every session. It is wise to keep them informed of the reasons for any deviation from normal attendance.

If you cannot attend all sessions of a course there are usually a few simple strategies which can help you gain access to the material covered. Reading the notes of a friend on the course is one strategy. Tutors will usually provide photocopies of any handouts or overhead transparencies, and sometimes it may be possible for a friend to audiotape a lecture (if the tutor agrees).

Whereas it is possible to catch up on some types of work which have been missed, it is harder to compensate for missing other aspects of a course. Normally it is not too difficult to read up aspects of a theory lecture, but laboratory or workshop exercises cannot easily be replicated at home. You cannot really compensate for the missed practical experience. Similarly, work experience is an area where it is difficult to compensate for missed attendance. There is an increasing number of courses which incorporate a placement in industry, commerce or overseas. This can last for a few weeks or up to one year. Usually, this period of work-based experience is an assessed part of the course. Such periods of experience often involve a commitment to an employer, and quite apart from the obligation to fulfil that commitment, it is not easy to replace the missed experience.

Two final points about attendance on courses. Attendance is not simply for the benefit of the individual student or of the institution, it is for the contribution which each student can make to the learning of others. We all learn a very great deal from our peers, and one of the most valuable experiences on a course is that gained from discussing issues in groups with other course members.

Finally, attendance on its own is not an absolute guarantee of progress on a course, nor of the learning of subject matter. Attendance is very much a means to an end, and that end is success on the course.

Summary

- If you are unable to meet all attendance requirements, discuss this with your tutor.
- There are many useful strategies to help compensate for missed sessions.
- If an organisation is paying your course fees, it is wise to keep them informed of changed attendance patterns.
- Lack of attendance at some types of sessions, e.g. work-based experience, is sometimes more difficult to compensate for.
- Attendance at courses enables you to contribute to the learning of your peers.

Setting up a learning group

In traditional agricultural societies learning was rarely separated from life itself. Children learned naturally about the planting, growing and harvesting cycles from their parents. There were no separate classes in agricultural science. In advanced industrial society, however, we have separated out the educational process and institutionalised it. As the complexity of life has increased and there has been a corresponding increase in the variety and quantity of knowledge which people need to absorb, there has tended to be a greater and greater emphasis upon institutionalised learning. We should not, however, underestimate the value of informal learning which takes place when small groups of people simply debate issues for the sheer love of discussion and conversation.

A group of people who travel on the same bus or train to work every morning will quite naturally read the morning paper and break into conversation about the latest political event. This kind of discussion and learning happens in the pub, in the workplace, at the sportsground and while parents are waiting for their children at school.

Some people take this kind of learning one step further and meet specifically to discuss a particular subject. People organise their own learning meetings to discuss the latest novel they have read; to discuss political or religious issues; to read poetry they have written; or to discuss ways of tracing their family history. Many of these interests are reflected through local societies and organisations.

The key point about informal learning groups is that they emphasise the importance of non-academic, everyday knowledge. It is easy for people to come to assume that this kind of knowledge is subservient to formally-acquired academic knowledge. In fact, even if we assume that there are two types of knowledge, they are both gained in the same way, i.e. from observation and experience. Very often academics use everyday knowledge gathered as questionnaires or interviews, and reconstitute it into academic knowledge. The latter is often more systematised and ordered, but it derives from the same basis.

The everyday knowledge which we possess is often of very great significance when compared with academic knowledge. This is particularly true in a subject such as history. Academics are able to create fairly precise chronologies of historical events, but it is a matter of debate as to whether this is a form which reveals the reality of a historical event or whether it brings it alive to people. On the other hand personal accounts by people who lived through historical events are often more real and give people a much more profound understanding. This is often seen most clearly with oral history. It is becoming increasingly common for researchers and academics to engage in long conversation with people (often the elderly) to discuss their experiences of events which took place when they were young. Such oral history can add enormously to the more conventional historical account. Autobiographical accounts are also extremely revealing. If we wanted to reach an understanding about the First World War we could read a formal historical account or we could read for example *Goodbye to All That* by Robert Graves. The latter may in some aspects be a rather subjective account, but it provides an immediacy and impact which is perhaps lacking in the formal textbook.

If you have a particular interest and want to set up an informal learning group, probably the best strategy is to attend meetings of a local club or society in a related area. You may then be able to make contact with a few people who share your specific interest. A local history society for instance, may enable you to make contact with people interested in tracing their family history. A local antiques society may enable you to set up a group interested in the history of Spode porcelain.

As you begin to establish yourselves as a learning group, you may want to set up outlets for your expertise. You could try to:

- Produce a newsletter which would enable group members to write short articles. This could be distributed free through public libraries.
- Offer to give talks on your specialist subject to local organisations.
- Write articles in magazines and journals.
- Make contact with similar groups in other parts of the country.

One final issue about learning groups is that while it may be very difficult to set up an informal learning group in an area like nuclear physics or biochemistry, there are certain subject areas where the major contribution to human learning is generated outside universities and colleges. An example is that of the creative arts such as creative writing and painting and sculpture. While these are studied in universities from an analytic viewpoint, the new and original art forms are created outside the academic environment. There is great scope to set up small groups to share experiences of writing and publishing poetry, jewellery making, painting, sculpture and writing novels and short stories. Not only can such groups be helpful as a forum for learning, but can also be a means of mutual support for creating a means for creative work to reach a wider audience. Jaques (1991) contains extensive advice on group learning.

Summary

- Informal, subjective knowledge is as valuable as academic knowledge.
- Learning groups set up outside the bounds of formal

institutions can be an equally valuable focus for learning and study.

■ In many areas of learning activity, e.g. creative arts, significant work is frequently located outside academic institutions.

Using college workshops

Colleges and universities are increasingly developing innovative ways of providing learning experiences. Although the lecture, tutorial and workshop still largely hold sway, there is a definite trend towards developing learning styles which place the impetus much more on the student to organise their own learning. The advent of computer-based learning has been a major factor in this regard, but there is now a focus upon creating collections of resource materials and encouraging students to work on their own, with access to a tutor when necessary.

The collections of learning materials are variously termed learning resource centres, learning workshops, or sometimes literacy or numeracy workshops if there is a specific subject focus. Most workshops are based in libraries, often because many of the materials such as CD-ROMs and reference books are already located there. However, the idea of a resource centre goes far beyond that of a conventional library. Additionally, there should be available:

■ Past examination papers and assignment questions for all the subjects covered by the workshop.

■ All of the necessary recommended texts used in the mainstream courses.

■ Handouts, self-teaching materials and software designed so that the student can make progress without the intervention of a tutor.

■ Practical learning aids for loan, such as calculators, rulers, compasses and protractors.

■ Video and audio tapes with headphones for private listening.

■ Examples of essays, problems and assignments with model answers.

■ Study skills guides to provide advice to students on using the workshop.

Although it should be possible to study and learn in the workshop without the assistance of a tutor, there should be a sufficient number of tutors available at least to provide advice on the location of materials.

Once such centres are set up they are generally less expensive for the college to run than providing conventional classes. This is mainly because there is a large reduction in the costs of staff payments. It is possible for more students to be learning with the presence of fewer staff.

A big advantage for the student is that you can drop in and drop out as you need to study. College workshops are usually open for extended periods and students can adjust their learning times to fit in between other commitments.

When using workshops you have to be prepared to adapt your learning to a situation where you will not have access to a tutor for most of the time. In a conventional class if you have difficulty with, say, a mathematics problem, the norm is to ask the tutor for assistance. In a workshop, on the other hand, the usual course of action is to work through examples and accompanying teaching materials yourself, and gradually acquire skills to solve the problem.

This type of learning process forces you to be:

- more self-reliant
- more determined
- more focused.

It may take you much longer, and you may have a number of false starts. However, success will almost certainly bring greater satisfaction and a sense of having achieved something. You should not feel that you cannot ask the tutor for help, but try to develop a sense of self-reliance in your own abilities.

Summary

- Use workshops to start and stop studying at your own convenience.
- Develop new independent ways of learning.
- Gain satisfaction from solving problems yourself.

4 | ORGANISING YOUR TIME

Using every spare moment

It is probably true that part-time students have to give much more attention to time management than full-time students. If you are working, have a family, have to care for an elderly relative, or have some other circumstance which prevents your studying full-time, then you almost certainly know the difficulties and frustrations of trying to do justice to your studies. Part-time, mature students often experience a variety of personal circumstances which make it difficult for them to progress with their studies at the rate they would like.

Most universities allow students to suspend their studies for a time, and this is one possibility. The other main strategy is to try to work around the commitments which you have, and by carefully managing your time make the most of the time you have available. This may sound as if it is underestimating the difficulties which some people have. This is certainly not so, but it seems to be the only positive approach to take.

It is also worth noting that other groups of students can have problems with time management. Paradoxically some students find that they actually have too much time for assignments. When there is an almost open-ended period in which to complete an assignment, this can sometimes bring its own pressures. You perhaps find that you take too long over a task which could be done adequately in a much shorter period of time. Full-time students may sometimes leave their assignments, and leave them and leave them until the time pressure builds up, and they then have to be very well organised to complete their work by the submission date.

Most people will admit to some problems with the management of time, and this is probably because we do not mind acknowledging that we could probably get a little more done if we used every minute to the full. One way to identify spare time is to carry out your own personal time audit.

You can do this for part of a day, a day, a week or a month. Having kept a careful record of how you spend literally every minute, you can then identify sections of time which you might have used to better advantage. You then try to learn from this in order to make the best use of time in the future. Here is a log of my own use of time for the six hours of a typical evening.

Time audit – evening

6.00	Arrive home from work.
6.00–6.15	Stand around in the kitchen chatting to the family and glancing at the television.
6.15–6.35	Go upstairs and change clothes. Look out of window thinking about the day's work. Decide what to do next.
6.35–6.55	Go down to kitchen and help with cooking dinner. Do some washing up. Chat to family.
6.55–7.20	Eat dinner with family while watching television.
7.20–8.00	Watch television, talk, sit in a bit of a daze.
8.00–8.20	Help with washing up.
8.20–8.30	Talk to children and make sure they have done their homework.
8.30–9.25	Do some preparation for tomorrow's teaching.
9.25	Feeling tired. Sit in front of television for five minute break.
10.00	Still sitting in front of television. Feel annoyed with myself.
10.00–10.30	Feed and walk the dogs.
10.30–11.00	Discuss the day with my wife.
11.00	Get work out again. Feeling tired.
11.30	Still managing to work, but feeling very, very tired.
11.45	Concentration lapsing. Pack up and go to bed, with vague feeling that the evening could have been used more productively.

Well that is a time audit for one of my evenings. Try making your own time audit. The important thing is to monitor your time carefully and accurately, and to record every little segment of time where there is a change of activity. The next step is to analyse the audit carefully in order to see where time savings can be made. In my own case, I decided that the television was the cause of my problems. I found that by simply not going near a television in the evenings, not only did I get more work done, but I had more time to talk to family members. However, you may not have the same experience, because time management is very personal. You may find that you can study very well with the television on in the same room. The main purpose of the time audit, however, is to help you identify ways in which you can reapportion your time more constructively.

Let us look at some things students say about time organisation:

'I break down what is needed to be studied and allot a percentage of time to be used each evening.'

'My main method is to divide the time that is spare to different tasks. The time is worked around the television and work.'

'I try to allocate specific times to specific tasks; e.g. on Friday I have no timetable, so I tend to work on projects in the workshops all day. On Thursday afternoons I have no timetable, so I usually work on the Pcs doing information technology work.'

'I try to do most of my studying in the evenings from about 6.30 onwards.'

'I tend to organise my time so that during the week I study during free time or in the evenings, so that I can leave the weekends free for the family.'

'I study whenever I have any spare time. I have to get my studies done in the evenings when the children are in bed.'

These students have obviously given thought to the organisation of their time, and try to make the most of their available time. One other way in which you can think of using time to the best advantage, is to consider the type of tasks which you do better at different times of the day. For example, you may find that writing is best done in the morning because you feel at your most clear-thinking and productive then. If you are writing later in the evening you may find that you need twice as much time to produce the same number of words. On the other hand, reading and note-taking may not be quite as demanding, and you may find that you can make good progress even in the evenings.

People almost certainly differ in the kinds of tasks which they perform better at different times of the day. The best guide here is to observe yourself carefully and try to match up the kind of studying you do, with the times you have available.

Summary

- Effective time management will improve your studying efficiency.
- Try keeping an audit of your use of time.
- Try to match the kind of studying you do with the time of the day best suited to you.

Making lists of priorities

Some students made a particular point about the need to have a series of priorities:

> 'I start by making lists and then I plan and prioritise the things which need doing.'
>
> 'I think about the projects that I have ongoing and then I rank them into orders of priority.'
>
> 'I try to prioritise my work, but it doesn't always work.'

Instead of discussing the need to prioritise in the abstract, let us consider a practical type of situation and discuss ways in which the separate tasks can be organised and prioritised. Let us suppose that you receive an assignment task sheet which outlines the following instructions for a piece of work.

Assignment

Design and carry out a small-scale investigation of the career aspirations of a group of college business studies students. You will need to make arrangements to collect data from a group of students, having obtained the necessary permission from the college authorities. You should decide on the reasons for selecting a particular group of students, and design the questionnaire or the interview schedule you will use. The report of the investigation should summarise some of the relevant literature and should draw clear conclusions from your study. The report should be about 2500 words in length. The submission date is six weeks from the date of this handout, i.e. the last session of term.

Probably the first decision which you need to make is to consider the college and the course which you will use as the focus for your research. If you were already a student in a different part of the same college, then it would be fairly straightforward to decide. You could probably gain access quite easily to information about Business Studies courses, and take a decision about the most appropriate course. You would want to know the number of students on the course in order to feel that you would be able to collect sufficient data. If you were going to a college with which you were unfamiliar, then you would need to consult their prospectus to gain information on the range of Business Studies courses.

In terms of taking decisions on priorities this has to be done first, because until you know the planned focus for the work, you cannot start to seek the permission necessary to carry out the data collection.

The next stage will be to consult the course tutor to ask permission to carry out the investigation and the data collection. You may do this by telephone or letter, but certainly if by the latter, there may be some time delay in obtaining a response. It is here that effective time management can be of assistance. While you are waiting for a reply you can be developing your questionnaire and/or interview schedule. In any case, if you make an appointment with the course tutor to arrange the actual process of data collection, then it would be helpful to have an example of the questionnaire at hand.

Now, it could even happen that the course tutor is away on holiday and there is a further time delay. There is not necessarily any need to waste this time. Although much of the finished report can only be written when you have collected and analysed the data, some of the introductory sections can be written at any time. You can certainly write the introduction which sets the scene and explains the overall purpose of the study. You can explain how you designed the investigation and how you came to use the particular group of students as respondents. You can also conduct an analysis of the relevant literature and select a number of extracts or quotations to use in your report. All of this can be done in the intervening time while perhaps you are awaiting another stage in the process.

When approaching an assignment task such as this then, it is clearly sensible to determine an action plan and a set of priorities. However it is also important to be creative about those priorities, and to amend them depending upon how things work out. You will then maximise your time and make best use of this scarce resource.

Summary

- Start by determining your order of priorities.
- Wherever possible have activities running in parallel so that you can interchange priorities.
- Move parts of tasks forwards and backwards in the list of priorities depending upon progress.

Planning your reading

A useful principle when thinking about making the best use of time when reading, is to link three important factors together. These three factors are the style of reading; the purpose of reading and the type of reading material. Unless these are matched to some extent, then you may not make the best use of time.

For example, let us suppose you are reading a chemistry textbook, and the purpose is to understand the chemical equations which summarise a particular group of reactions. However, you try to achieve this by simply scanning the pages. It is unlikely with this style of reading that you will achieve your purpose. You would simply not be concentrating in sufficient detail on the equations to extend your understanding.

A different example is, say, the reading of a novel where the main purpose is relaxation and enjoyment. If you were to concentrate on the syntax of the sentences and the finer points of grammatical construction, then you would probably find that you did not enjoy the novel very much. You would not have sufficient time to think about the plot and the main characters.

Of course, works of literature such as short stories, poems, novels and plays can be read for a variety of purposes. They can be read for pleasure, but they can also be read for a number of other reasons. They can be studied in terms of the style of language used, the vocabulary, and for references which place them in a particular historical or social context. If you are reading a work as part of a course in literature, then you will also probably be examining certain passages in detail and considering their meaning and relevance. You may be trying to memorise some quotations, and thinking carefully about leading characters and about the possible motivation for their actions. While you are engaged in this detailed study you may also be enjoying what you are reading, but clearly you are not reading primarily for entertainment.

Some types of reading material are such that you may spend a good deal of time and yet only read a very small amount of material. A mathematics textbook may belong to this category, where the reader may spend several hours going over and over a single worked example in order to understand it.

Some books demand a particular kind of reading style. A good example are books with illustrations, such as fine art books or some history books. Here the text usually makes constant reference to the illustrations and it is important to give as much attention to the latter as to the text. It is often necessary to study the text, move to the relevant illustration, and then go back and re-read the text.

Sometimes it is not the purpose of reading to collect as much knowledge as possible. It is sufficient to scan read something in order to gain an overview or to select the key concepts being used. This type of reading can cover a considerable amount of material in a fairly short time. A totally different style and purpose is involved where the ultimate goal is to cram sufficient knowledge in order to pass an examination. Such reading will tend to be slower and more methodical and will probably need to be supplemented with strategies such as note-taking.

Reading, however, is like any skill. It can be improved. Whereas techniques may not have a dramatic effect, they can be very useful in developing the reading process. Here are two of many techniques which may help you improve reading. The first is to help you identify the key concepts in a piece of writing, and the second is generally to improve your level of understanding and appreciation of a passage.

Technique 1

For this you need a serious newspaper or journal article and a black felt-tip pen. Read the article once and then go back deleting all of the phrases and sentences which are not central to the arguments or do not seem to be key concepts. When this is done you should have simply the main ideas standing out from the passage. This is a good exercise to help you focus on the main points in a passage.

Technique 2

Another way of maximising your time when reading and studying is to plan to teach someone what you have learned. This may sound a rather strange idea, but the discipline of having to explain a topic to someone else ensures that you have to get your ideas into order and present them systematically. You may find that the exercise works best when you need to read a difficult passage or topic, and you know that you are going to have difficulty in absorbing the information and ideas. Ask a friend to allow you to explain the ideas to them. It would probably help if they have a certain level of understanding in the subject because they could then ask you questions which would further test your knowledge. Once you have read the passage, make a few brief notes and then give a short explanation to your friend. This need only last a few minutes, but it will quickly demonstrate to you the limits of your knowledge.

The act of teaching and explaining something will make certain demands upon you such as:

1 It will force you to pick out the key ideas of a topic and to compose your own understanding of how they link together.

2 When you describe something happening (whether an event in a laboratory or a social event) you will have to consider a plausible explanation. Your friend may ask you why something has happened and you will need an answer!

3 You will very quickly learn where the gaps in your knowledge and understanding exist. You may find that you fumble over your explanation or that your account does not seem as coherent as you would like. The result of this is that you will know immediately the parts which you need to re-read and understand more deeply.

This may sound a rather lengthy way of organising your time properly. However, if you are having difficulty in understanding something, you may spend hours and hours reading a passage, or part of a book and not make much progress. The need to explain the topic will really focus your mind.

Summary

■ When you are reading, try to match the style of reading, the purpose of reading, and the type of reading material. This will enable you to read more efficiently and maximise your use of time.

■ Practise eliminating the supporting material in a piece of text, and concentrating on the main ideas.

■ Practise reading about a topic and then teaching it to a friend.

Creating study periods

One of the rather strange things about studying is that different people appear to work better in a variety of different situations. Some people seem to work very effectively when there is loud music playing, while others are capable of driving themselves through considerable sleep deprivation in order to complete an assignment on time. The students who provided opinions and comments for this book clearly showed that there is an almost endless variety of techniques employed when studying. Rather than assuming that one technique is absolutely the best, we need to become careful observers of our own aptitudes and approaches to study. We need to study ourselves and our own learning styles, and then match the kind of activity we undertake to the time of the day and the situation.

One way to do this is to plan, say, one week at a time and to anticipate as far as possible the periods which are available for study. Write these time periods down on the left-hand side of a page. Then list on the right-hand side, the different study tasks which you need to complete in the week, matching them as far as possible to the most appropriate time for yourself. When doing this think carefully about the tasks which you feel you could accomplish best at certain times in the week. Your chart might look something like Figure 4.1.

Monday

| 5.00 pm–6.00 pm | Plan out next assignment |
| 6.00 pm–7.00 pm | Revise origins of First World War |

Tuesday

| 6.30 pm–7.30 pm | Learn French vocabulary |

Wednesday

| 8.00 pm–10.00 pm | Practise use of spreadsheets on computer |

Figure 4.1 Specimen study plan

The planning of the next assignment has been allocated to an early time in the evening, on the assumption that it needs a good deal of creative thinking when the mind is not too tired. Learning and revision work has been scheduled for the middle part of the evenings. The practice of computer skills however, has been placed later in the evening, on the assumption that it is perhaps a slightly more relaxing activity. These assumptions may not be true for you, but the main thing is to reflect on the best times for you to carry out certain kinds of activities. This should not only help you organise your time, but use it to the best effect.

Summary

- Try to plan ahead the study periods for the week, and also the tasks which need doing.
- Match the tasks to the study periods so that you are doing the activity which you perform best at that time of the day.

Becoming task-oriented

Study is a very achievement-oriented activity. Even if we are just studying something for pleasure, the assumption is usually that we want to make significant progress; to learn more about it; be able to discuss the subject and have the satisfaction of understanding it. If we are working towards a qualification then we will probably have a lot of ready-made tasks to achieve. Assignments must be submitted and term papers prepared.

However, we can probably make our study activities more efficient by identifying competences which we do not possess or would like to improve, and making a conscious effort to develop them. A study competence can be thought of as a practical skill which helps you to achieve the tasks necessary to progress and succeed. Examples of study competences might be:

The ability to use a desk-top publishing package to design and prepare an assignment cover sheet.

- The ability to arrange a sequence of references in alphabetical order automatically using a computer.
- The ability to prepare a journal article in the required format for publication.

- The ability to link together the names and ideas of a large number of theorists when discussing a topic, or writing an essay.
- The ability to concentrate on studying for long periods at a time when necessary.
- The ability to write clear, grammatical English.
- The ability to speak confidently and articulately in a seminar group.

We often get ideas for competences we would like to acquire by watching other students or colleagues and noting the things they can do well. It is very important though when we are doing this, that we do not feel inferior when making comparisons. After all, there are almost certainly things you can do which other people cannot do. However, we can learn an enormous amount simply by watching others and deciding which competences we wish to acquire. This is the first essential stage in becoming task-oriented.

Deciding what we want to learn is one thing, but finding a way to develop that competence is another. It can often seem as if some of our peers do things quite naturally when we really have to struggle. Speaking in group situations is an example, as indicated at the end of the above list. Being able to express ourselves in group or public situations is an important competence in relation to studying. For example:

- We may need to attend an interview in order to gain a place on a course.
- Some assignments involve giving a talk or presentation.
- Some advanced courses (e.g. research degrees) are partly assessed by oral examination (called a viva).
- Some teaching is carried out in tutorials and seminars, and students are expected to contribute ideas.
- You may need to ask questions in lectures in order to understand a topic better.
- You may be a student representative on a course, and need to represent the views of fellow students at course committee meetings.
- You may be interviewed by the external examiner for a course and need to answer questions about your work.

The main question is though, in what way do you acquire a study competence? How do you go about enhancing skills when perhaps there is no specific course devoted to them? Indeed these are the very competences which underpin and support the course you are doing. There are, of course, many strategies, including learning from peers, but perhaps a key approach to try is learning by increments. This involves setting out to progress in very small stages, which, each taken in turn, is non-threatening and unlikely to induce any feeling of stress.

Learning to be confident and articulate in public situations is an example. If you do not feel very happy in such situations it is unlikely that you will be able to make a long speech the first time of trying. It is much better to start with a short contribution.

Try asking the lecturer or speaker a question. However it is not always easy to formulate one, and we do not always want to ask a question which suggests we have not understood anything that was said. Why not try saying:

> 'Would you mind expanding a little on what you said about ...?'
>
> Could you recommend any further reading on ...?'

These are non-contentious questions and comments, and would give you experience of speaking in a group. A second stage would be to add to something which has already been said. Listen to the comments which other students make and then see if these prompt thoughts in your own mind. Then you could say something such as:

> 'Just to add to what John was saying earlier ...'
>
> 'Further to the comment just made by Jane ...'

Finally you will probably find that you develop the confidence to contribute your own comments. This incremental approach can be applied to the learning of many tasks or competences. It is a matter of taking your learning in stages and achieving what you can realistically manage. In this way you will improve your study competences in a variety of ways.

Summary

- ■ Try to identify competences which will improve your ability to study.
- ■ Divide the learning of these competences into different tasks.
- ■ Practise using an incremental approach to learning new skills.

Reading assessment schedules

Assessment is probably one of the most important parts of any course of study. It is the point at which the student discovers the standard or quality of his or her work. It is also when the teacher allocates a particular grade or mark and also, perhaps, recommends the award of a qualification.

Before we look in detail at formal assessment, however, it is worth remembering (particularly in the context of time management) that assessment is a fairly general term and can be applied in a variety of situations.

Firstly there is self-assessment. It is important to learn to evaluate our own work. Admittedly this is not always easy, because we may not quite be able to distance ourselves from it. However if we know the criteria by which the assignment is being judged, then we should be able to evaluate the weak points and strong points of the piece of work. It can save a lot of time in terms of later corrections, if we take a reflective look at our work as it progresses.

Peer assessment is another valuable process whereby other course members read or listen to your work and make comments about it. This kind of process can be valuable for all group members, as each person can gain ideas for the improvement of their own work. On some courses, peer assessment is an integral part of the course, whereby for example, seminar papers are delivered to a peer group and members comment upon them. For this to work well it does require a supportive attitude on the part of the group members. Again peer assessment can provide useful feedback which can save valuable time in preparing an assignment.

Neither self-assessment nor peer assessment are normally part of the formal assessment of course work which is associated with the awarding of grades, but can be regarded as supplementary and supportive.

However, the formal assessment requirements of a unit or module should be set down precisely in a course document which is available for all students to read. This is important because it is crucial that you understand what you need to do to complete an assignment and also the criteria which will be used to assess the work. Understanding these issues before you start work on an assignment can help you to organise your time efficiently because you know exactly what you need to do. You do not waste time on unnecessary activities.

The kind of information available to you before you start work on an assignment should include the following:

- A clear statement of the work you must produce i.e. an essay; a seminar paper; or a portfolio.
- The length of the assignment.
- The date for submission.
- How and where to submit the assignment.
- An example of a blank, tutor assessment sheet.
- The criteria to be used when assessing the assignment. These might include both general and specific criteria.
- Whether the assignment will be graded.
- In what way the assignment may contribute to the overall course grade or classification.

Some of these issues are very important when it comes to managing your study time. Fundamentally it is important to know what is expected of you. You may be set an essay to write, but once you start work on it you may be unclear whether you are expected to provide examples of empirical data; to what extent you should refer to research studies; and how long the bibliography should be. Some of the issues may be addressed in the assessment schedule, but if not you will need to seek clarification from your tutor.

The length of the assignment should be stated precisely. There appear to be a number of ways in which tutors habitually express this, for example:

- about 5000 words in length
- not more than 5000 words in length
- between 4000 words and 6000 words
- 5000 words ± 10%
- about 5000 to 6000 words

The way in which the length of an assignment is expressed can cause some confusion, not only with regard to the actual length required but also whether the bibliography and abstract should be included. In order to avoid misunderstandings it is worth clarifying such issues with your tutor.

The more you know about what is expected of you, the better you can organise your time and the less likely you are to waste time on unnecessary work. If you know that for a particular length piece of work, a list of references of about twenty items is considered reasonable, then you can aim for that. All of this information may not be on the assessment schedule you are given, and it would be best to get further clarification.

Summary

- Self-assessment and peer assessment are valuable in providing developmental advice.
- Formal assessment requirements are usually set down in an assessment schedule, which can help you to plan your work efficiently.

Judging the length of assignments

The length of an assignment is something which should be considered carefully. On one level, if you write much more than is required then you are simply doing too much work! This will obviously take up valuable time that perhaps could be used to advantage on another part of the course. Tutors give considerable thought to assignment lengths, and often there is a reasonable degree of uniformity about what is expected from course to course in an institution. Some of the important reasons for allocating a word length to assignments are as follows:

- It makes it possible to calculate accurately the total assessment requirement of a course, and to compare this with similar courses.
- It gives an indication of the amount of detail and depth of argument required.
- It imposes a discipline upon the student to express ideas within a particular space.
- It enables students to manage their time in terms of study.
- It enables tutors to manage their time in terms of marking.

One of the great difficulties with academic writing is to be able to judge the quantity of detail to put into an essay or other assignment. As you move on to higher level courses there is a tendency to take more and more for granted in terms of the reader. While at school you will include all the basic facts and arguments about a subject. At college you will omit some of these, assuming that there is no need to restate them, and you will concentrate on the more sophisticated issues. This kind of process of elimination continues at each level.

Therefore, within a certain level and length of assignment there is always a series of decisions to be taken about what you should include and what you should leave out. This is especially important when writing essays under examination conditions.

Given an assignment of unlimited length and an infinite amount of time to complete it, presumably all of the available information in existence could be included. As we reduce the assignment to realistic limits, we have to be selective and exercise judgement about what to include. It is normally sensible to include the most sophisticated arguments of which we are aware in the subject area, and to present these within a rational structure. The best strategy is to divide up the assignment into sections determined either by the structure of the question, or by imposing a logical structure on the topic. Knowing the overall assignment length, word limits can be imposed on each section. However, depending upon the extent and depth of the information to be included in each section, judgements will need to be made about the distribution of the total number of words.

It is also worth finding out from your tutors whether there are any informal expectations about stated word lengths. For example, if an assessment schedule says that the anticipated word length for an assignment is 5000 to 7000 words, this may mean a variety of things.

It may suggest that in reality tutors are expecting a 6000 word assignment, but are indicating a certain amount of flexibility. On the other hand, it may signify that 7000 words is the norm, and that in fact 5001 words would be considered really much too short. You need to clarify such issues with your tutor. Sometimes there is a mismatch between the assessment schedule and the expectations of tutors.

In any case, 7000 words is actually longer than 5000 words by a factor of 40%. This is a major difference and represents an opportunity for a student to go into much greater detail and hence arguably get a much better grade.

Some courses specify the limits by which a word length may be exceeded or by which the student may fall short. Occasionally, there is a penalty in terms of grades for students who stray too far from the recommended length. The argument in assessment terms is that the assessor is not comparing like with like if students move too far from the word limit. As discussed above, the student who writes more has the opportunity to include more lengthy and perhaps more complex arguments. If penalties are involved then clearly the message is to adhere to the word limits.

Summary

- The length of assignments is a measure of the depth and complexity of information which should be included.
- Length of assignment imposes a discipline on the writer which is an important part of academic writing.
- Exceeding the specified word length may incur an assessment penalty.

Working towards submission dates

Submission dates for assignments are not invented by tutors simply to be unpleasant! They serve a number of functions on a course:

- They ensure that students tend to progress through a course steadily, completing their work in sequence.
- Like word lengths, they impose a sense of discipline on study, so that students do not continue preparing an assignment for an unlimited period.
- They are part of the structure of a course, enabling the tutors to coordinate the curriculum and units of study.
- They are an important part of the assessment process enabling assessors and examiners to plan their work.
- They enable the end date of a course to be carefully planned, and for students and tutors to both know when the pass list can be published and the awards ceremony held.

This is a fairly impressive list of justifications and it is therefore quite important that you try to stick to submission dates. Employing many of the time management skills outlined earlier in the book, should ensure that you are reasonably on target. It is also important, however, to guard against last-minute problems which can throw the best-laid plans into disarray.

Photocopiers tend to break down and the page numbers of your assignment seem to go wrong on your computer disc! No matter what precautions you take, there always seems to be a problem, no matter how slight. It is obviously a good idea to allow for these mishaps and to leave a certain amount of time free before the submission date.

It is also worth considering the actual process of submission. It was often the case that assignments would be handed in to a tutor on the last session of a course. This worked well unless there was an unfortunate event like an assignment going missing or a dispute over whether or not it had actually been handed in at all.

Nowadays many tutors have developed systems whereby receipts are given when work is handed in, and whereby the student signs for work when it is returned after assessment. Another common strategy is to use a postbox system within the college, whereby all assignments must be posted by a certain time and date. When the postbox is opened there is no ambiguity over whether an assignment has been submitted or not.

If you feel that you will not manage to complete an assignment by the submission date, the main strategy should be to communicate with your tutor. If you do not do this, the tutors on the course may assume that you have decided to leave the course, and they certainly cannot implement any steps to help you. If you do explain to them your difficulties, there are a number of steps they can take:

- If you are having difficulty with part of the assignment they may be willing to give you general advice without feeling that they have given you an unfair advantage over other students.

- If you need a little extra time, they may be able to formally give you an extension and a revised submission date.

- If you feel that you cannot complete the work at the moment, nor in the near future, they may arrange a formal deferral, which means that you will have a rest and restart the unit or course at a later date. This will take the pressure off you, and enable you to restart when you feel able.

However all of this requires communication, so make sure you talk to your tutor!

Summary

- Submission dates provide a target for you and also help the course to run smoothly.

- Leave time for the possibility of late mishaps just before submission of your assignment.

- Ask for a dated receipt when you hand in your assignment.

- If you are having problems, the golden rule is 'talk to your tutor.'

5 | IMPROVING YOUR STUDY TECHNIQUES

Communicating with your tutor

If you are enrolled on a formal academic course then you will possibly be allocated a personal tutor and, of course, you will be taught by a range of specialist subject tutors. For the duration of your course and perhaps for some time afterwards, these people will be very significant in your life. However, many students just see their tutors as people who lecture to them and who perhaps hand them back their assessed work. They often fail to see the 'person' behind the tutor.

The first thing to be said about tutors is that it is their job to know what they are doing when it comes to academic matters. They have been appointed because of their academic qualifications, and because of a range of other experience including industrial or commercial experience, training, teaching or research. They also may have wide experience of publishing, editing or writing. You may not always realise it, but some of your tutors may have a national or international reputation in their subject field.

Moreover, because they are well-qualified they will have been through the same kind of course that you are now following. They have had to study and write essays; they have had to give tutorial papers and they have had to defend a dissertation in an oral examination. It is likely that they were good at these things because they need to be well-qualified to gain an academic teaching post. All of this may sound like singing the praises of lecturers! It is not intended to read like that, but rather to point out an obvious but perhaps easily overlooked fact that tutors have an immense fund of knowledge and expertise on academic matters, only part of which generally shows itself in formal lectures. It is clearly a good idea to try to take advantage of this source of help.

Apart from subject expertise, your tutors have access to a very wide range of knowledge and contacts such as:

■ They are able to provide good advice on doing assignments. They know what is expected and what makes a good assignment.

■ They understand the way the university or college functions and they are broadly familiar with the range of courses offered.

■ They usually have professional contacts in other colleges and in other countries.

■ They may have national roles such as being Chief Examiners or external examiners at other universities.

■ They write and edit books.

■ They are familiar with the wide range of literature in your subject area.

Lecturers are involved in education usually because they are very interested in their subject area and because they enjoy teaching and helping students. It seems only sensible to use some of this willingness to help in order to assist you in your studies.

The advice of your tutors on assignments is very important because they know what is expected. They will probably mark your assignments anyway. There may, of course, be other markers and almost certainly an external examiner, but your tutor will be involved in the process and hence will be very much aware of what is required. One or two of your tutors may also be employed for example as examiners or markers for National Examination Boards. Alternatively, they may act themselves as external examiners to other universities, ensuring the quality of their awards and moderating some of their students' assignments. This kind of activity means that they are very much aware of the national situation with regard to your type of course and qualification.

Tutors often feel (quite rightly) that they must limit somewhat the specificity of the advice they give on assignments, otherwise there is a danger that it becomes more of their work than yours. However, it is a good idea to consider carefully the advice which they do give.

Tutors can be very useful to you through their general knowledge of the Higher Education system. If you wanted to do a short course in another department they would be able to offer advice or to put you in contact with a colleague who may be able to help you. Lecturers often have very wide networks of contacts in universities both in this country and overseas, and can put this network at your disposal to help you. They can find out about scholarships and student exchanges and opportunities to study abroad. They can also often help you publish some of your own writing. They can help you rework a good project into a form which might be suitable for a journal article, and they can advise you where to send it. If they are editing a book, they may offer you the chance to write a chapter. Alternatively, they can put you in touch with publishers who might be willing to consider a rewriting of a project or dissertation.

You cannot take advantage of this kind of advice unless you know your tutors and they know you. It is very difficult for lecturers to get to know you during formal lectures. The groups are usually large and there just is not sufficient time to remember everyone's name. Equally, it is not always easy to go up to your lecturer at the end and introduce yourself. Tutorials do help, if these are part of your course.

However, there is nothing to stop you introducing yourself if you see your tutor around college, and perhaps asking a short question. Also, your tutor will probably tell you where his or her room is, to enable you to hand in work, and they will probably not mind if you call to ask for some brief advice. The main rule is not to stay more than a few minutes because they are likely to be busy with administration or writing. However, it is very useful for tutors to meet their students, because it is a very good way of obtaining feedback, and learning about the course from the student's point of view.

A final way in which tutors can be very helpful is in providing feedback on assignments. There is a tendency when you receive your assessment sheet to simply concentrate on the grade or mark awarded and not to try to reflect upon the comments. Obviously tutors do vary in their style of comments. Some will concentrate on the limitations of the work as they see them; others might try to write encouraging comments; while others may try to suggest specific ways in which future assignments may be improved. Perhaps a combination of all three approaches is most useful. Here is what some students said about the significance of feedback on assignments:

'Feedback is very important. I like written comments followed by a discussion with the tutor.'

'It sometimes feels as if feedback always comes too late, because I am already working on the next assignment.'

'A discussion with a tutor about an assignment can be very useful for pinpointing problem areas. Written comments as a backup are very helpful for future reference.'

'When I am getting feedback I prefer written comments. I don't want to be told my assignment is rubbish to my face! It might be embarrassing!'

'The best kind of feedback is the sort that offers an insight into what bits have been missed, rather than a critique of what is there.'

'Feedback is crucial especially in initial assignments in order to determine the level the lecturer is expecting.'

There are a number of interesting and important issues which emerge from these student comments. It is very important for example, to get feedback from your tutor before you start on the next assignment. This seems so logical that one wonders why it does not always happen automatically. In fact, it can be that assignments overlap for all kinds of reasons. A common factor is that assignment comment sheets have to be held back until an external examiner has approved the grades. This can mean that the next assignment is completed before you receive comments about the previous one. If you suspect that this is likely to happen, then visit your tutor and ask for at least some oral feedback to guide you with the next piece of work.

When they are marking work tutors sometimes take a holistic view when writing comments. They look at the piece of work in general, and make some broad statements about its virtues and negative qualities. It is, however, very important for students to have precise guidance on what they have omitted, or shortcomings in their arguments. If you feel that the comments on your work are not sufficiently specific, then ask for precise advice which can be used to try for a higher grade in future.

Having commented at some length on how useful tutors can be, it is important to remember that if occasionally you have a genuine complaint to make, then you should definitely make it. You are entitled to the very best tuition, to care and consideration, and to prompt advice from your tutor. However, if you can at all, it is always best to mention it to your tutor personally. If you make your comment politely, most tutors will remedy the error very quickly. Often it can be a misunderstanding or that they did not appreciate the consequences of their actions. However, you may not feel able to do this, and fortunately there is usually a mechanism which saves face all round, and yet has the desired effect.

Most courses have provision for a student representative elected by the students, who sits on the course committee and can make comments. The purpose of this arrangement is specifically to provide a route for student comments (whether positive or negative) to be heard. If you feel that a tutor or tutors could improve arrangements or teaching in some way, you can let your course representative know. The advantages of this are threefold:

1 You can then find out from your representative if you are the only student who has this particular opinion, or whether others have mentioned it as well.

2 You can express your opinion honestly knowing that the tutor concerned will not find out who you are. The representative can report directly to the tutor, in a calm, objective way.

3 The tutor is not faced with a public complaint, but has the opportunity to respond to the complaint through the representative as intermediary.

Such a system benefits both the students and the tutor.

Summary

■ Get to know your tutors and try to take advantage of their knowledge and experience.

■ Lecturers have specific expertise in terms of advice on doing assignments, and knowing the standards which should be reached.

■ If necessary ask your tutors for additional feedback on assignments.

■ If you have a complaint about the standard of lecturing or
some other related matter, try to put the issue to your tutor
anonymously, using your course representative as an
intermediary.

Getting the most from lectures

When asked whether lectures were an effective means of promoting
learning, one student replied:

> 'How much I learn from a lecture depends on the person giving
> the lecture.'

This simple statement may strike many of you as being very true. Most
students have probably sat through some lectures which were boring and
uninformative, while other lectures were inspirational. It often seems
when it comes to the interest-value of a lecture, as if the subject matter is
less important than the charisma-level of the lecturer. Although we could
easily list a number of characteristics of an interesting lecturer, what we
are trying to develop in this section are a series of strategies to ensure that
whoever is lecturing, you are able to help create an interesting learning
experience.

The words 'help create' are important here. The key argument of this
section is that you as a student can help create the type of lecture you
want, even if your lecturer does not do this naturally. The main feature of
a lecture is communication, and two-way communication is much better
than one-way communication.

Sometimes lecturers will explain before they begin, that they welcome
questions and comments and actually dislike having to deliver long
monologues. This approach will probably ensure an interesting dialogue
and good communication between tutor and students. On the other hand,
if the lecturer simply starts talking and transmitting information, after a
while this can seem tedious. There is nothing to stop you asking a few
questions:

- 'Excuse me, could you go back to the point you mentioned earlier, and explain that again?'
- 'Do you have any special references to recommend for this issue?'
- 'Excuse me, are there any alternative perspectives to this?'
- 'Do some academics take a different view to this one?'

These last two questions are very useful, if you feel that the lecturer is spending a lot of time concentrating on one particular viewpoint. Generally, academics are good in lectures at portraying different arguments about an issue, because they are trained to do this. However, occasionally some lecturers do tend to be a bit repetitive about a personally-favoured viewpoint. The main point is to engage the lecturer in debate and communication. The lecture experience will almost certainly be more interesting.

The structure of a room or lecture theatre can have a big effect upon the levels of communication. Sometimes you will not be able to move the furniture, but if you can then experiment with different layouts. A series of rows for example, is much more likely to generate a highly-formal lecture. A circle or semi-circle encourages more democratic, participative discussion. You can always ask the lecturer to alter the layout.

When asking a lecturer questions, it is a good idea not to be too challenging in either the style or content of the question, for example:

- 'Surely that theory isn't the only one which can be applied to this?'
- 'I have been reading about this alternative view – why haven't you covered that?'

This is not to suggest that lecturers always deserve students to be kind and nice to them. Rather it is to point out that lecturers are like everyone in situations when they are on show – they can feel rather vulnerable. You want to have the most interesting and informative lecture possible, and the way to achieve this is to be as encouraging and supportive of your lecturer as seems reasonable.

Perhaps the biggest danger in lectures, especially large lectures in lecture theatres, is that you find yourself not concentrating for large periods. It is not easy to concentrate for much more than about twenty minutes at a time, and it is easy to find yourself allowing your mind to drift away from the subject of the lecture. If this happens on a regular basis you may inadvertently be falling behind in your studies without realising it. Unless there is very regular assessment you may have no indication that you are not really keeping up with your learning. This can be particularly serious in some subjects which are accumulative in their learning, such as languages and mathematics; i.e. you cannot understand the next stage without having completely understood the previous stage. The best strategy to avoid loss of attention is to keep mentally active in the lecture by making notes, drawing diagrams and asking questions. If you do find yourself having lost concentration, then try to read up on what you have missed once the lecture is over.

Summary

- You can influence the teaching style of the lecturer and the degree of participation in the lecture.
- Ask questions whenever you need clarification.
- Ask to change the layout of the room if it is not conducive to good communication.
- Try to develop strategies to minimise lapses in concentration.

Learning from tutorials

The word tutorial can be used to refer to several slightly different types of learning situations. It is normally used to describe a one-to-one meeting between a tutor and a student, but can also refer to a tutor meeting with a small group of students. The tutorial can have one or more of several different purposes:

- To enable the tutor to review for the student the latter's performance in an assignment.
- An informal teaching situation to enable the tutor to expand on issues previously covered in lectures.
- A general discussion to enable the tutor to check on a student's progress on a course.
- To enable the tutor to offer advice on a specific project, or thesis.

From a student's viewpoint, there are probably two main general aims for a tutorial. These are:

- To learn from the tutor; to ask questions and be offered advice; and to understand what is expected for a particular assignment.
- To demonstrate to the tutor what the student has learned, and what progress has been made.

It is very useful to prepare well for tutorials, and perhaps even to write down a list of questions to ask them. This can be helpful because the tutor may in fact be leaving it up to you to lead the tutorial. He or she may assume you have come with a series of questions to raise. If you find yourself a little short of questions then think of the current assignment you are doing and any difficulties you are having. You may as well use your tutor as a repository of good advice while you have access to him or her.

Remember to use the tutorial as an opportunity to demonstrate your own knowledge and understanding of your subject. The skill of being able to argue coherently about your subject is very important, particularly if you apply for another course at some stage. Your tutor will also probably be involved in writing a reference for you at some point, and the impression gained in tutorials is important in influencing what will be written.

A very important function of tutorials is to give you feedback on your progress. One student summed this up by saying:

> 'I like one-to-one tutorials because I can get confirmation if I am doing OK.'

Clearly you will get feedback on your grades on assignment sheets, but unless results are published on a notice board, you may not know how well you are doing in comparison with other course members. Your tutor may be willing to give you an overview of your progress on the course, and an indication of how well you are doing in comparison with others.

In many colleges and universities you may find that you are allocated a personal tutor whose role it is to look after your general welfare, both academic and personal, during your course. Personal tutors generally interpret their role with different degrees of enthusiasm and sense of duty, but you can always ask for a change of tutor if you are unhappy. A good personal tutor can help you enormously, particularly at those times of crisis when, for example, you want to change your option at the last minute. Your personal tutor can act as an advocate for you and help you find your way through the maze of the academic bureaucracy.

Finally a tutorial is a very good opportunity to express enthusiasm for your course (if you are genuinely enjoying it) and to say you have enjoyed your tutor's lectures (if that is so)! This may seem a rather awkward thing to do, particularly as the culture at school is not to do this kind of thing very much. However, it is more common in Higher Education where students and tutors know each other perhaps a little better. Tutors do like to be told if their students enjoy their lectures. Tutors are like everyone else, in that they sometimes lack confidence and wonder whether they are doing a good job. A small compliment from a student can brighten up a lecturer's day and reinforce those aspects of teaching which are going down well with students. The reverse is also true. It is important for tutors to use tutorials to compliment students on the work done well. This can act as reinforcement and motivation. When it comes to studying and learning, nothing succeeds like success!

Summary

- Go to tutorials well-prepared to ask questions and to gain the most from the tutorial.
- Use tutorials to demonstrate your own understanding of your subject.
- Ask your tutor for an assessment of your overall progress.
- Use your personal tutor to help you if you have difficulties or uncertainties.

Learning by discussing

Learning by discussing is one of the oldest forms of learning. It was used a great deal by the ancient Greeks and has passed down in the philosophical tradition so that it is one of the main ways in which philosophers try to resolve conceptual problems.

The process involves one person making a claim or assertion that something is true or that something is the case. The other person will then think of a reason why this cannot be so, or perhaps they will think of a contrary example. The first person then tries to nullify that argument, and so the process continues. It may be that this process will never arrive at 'the truth' about something, and arguably this is an impossibility anyway. However, it should result in a rather more precise understanding of an issue, and an enhanced conceptual clarification. For example, we might take the case of euthanasia, which is a subject much subjected to ethical analysis. A discussion around this issue might proceed as follows:

Person A: I think euthanasia is always wrong because it involves taking human life and that is murder.

Person B: Yes, I agree it involves taking life and that is not a pleasant thought. However, a person's quality of life may have become so poor that they would prefer to die.

Person A: All right, can you give me an example?

Person B: Yes. Imagine a person with cancer who is in great pain, and says 'please give me a drug overdose to end my misery; I would rather die than suffer like this'.

Person A: Well, I have several answers to that. Firstly, they may recover. This may seem unlikely but it can happen. If we kill them (and that is what it is) then we will never know if recovery was possible.

Secondly, we have another option. We have a wide range of pain killers which we can administer.

Thirdly, there is the problem of the person who will administer the drugs overdose. Notwithstanding the legal position, somebody would have to be found to carry out the deed.

Fourthly, we can all get very depressed when we are in pain. Today we may wish ourselves dead, whereas tomorrow things may seem slightly better and we are reasonably happy to be alive.

Person B: Yes I agree there are difficulties. However, is there not an issue of personal freedom here? If I am very ill and in pain, but I can get about, I can choose whether or not to end my life. I can get the means to kill myself. On the other hand, if I am ill in bed and cannot move, I may have to suffer for years because I cannot gain the means to die. Should not society provide me with the means to end my suffering?

Person A: Well imagine a society where you could have a euthanasia pill on request. Perhaps you could get them at the chemist. Everytime you felt really fed up or had a really bad migraine you might consider ending it all. There would be cases of euthanasia all over the place. In any case, how could you distinguish between 'mercy killing' and murder. The whole thing could be very badly misused.

At this point we can perhaps leave the argument with a feeling that perhaps Person B is getting slightly the worse of it. However, Person B may not feel like that and may be perfectly happy to continue developing his or her argument. An alternative is that either disputant can come to the conclusion that they have pressed one particular line of argument too far, and can say in effect: 'All right, you have a good point there, but let's return to that issue I mentioned earlier.' In other words they concede one line of argument but want to revert to another possibility and see how that develops. It is rather like two chess players who have agreed a draw but who trace back the game to explore different variations and see who would have won under different conditions.

The main idea about this type of discussion is that it is not conducted in a competitive spirit, but rather in a spirit of enquiry. The purpose is not to win as such, but to enjoy the pursuit of 'truth'. We recognise that the latter is unattainable, but it provides a hypothetical ideal after which we can strive.

When this kind of debate is conducted in a competitive spirit, in order to 'win the argument' or 'put the other person down', it defeats the object and ultimately can descend into rather crude point-scoring. Unfortunately much of the debate which we hear is of this kind. Whenever you find yourself in this kind of discussion, it is necessary to keep reminding others that 'we are not trying to win here, just analyse the issue'.

A good tutor can often manage to 'referee' an excellent debate in a small group seminar for example. When you are a member of such a discussion it is a very pleasant experience both intellectually and socially. Everyone loses themselves in the argument (the intellectual argument not a dispute). The more you can engage in this kind of learning experience the better, but it often demands a serious attempt on the part of participants to work together rather than against each other.

If you do find yourself in a study group where things are getting a little out of hand, and where the spirit of cooperation has been lost, it is a good idea to develop one or two groundrules and to put these forward for agreement by the group. There are many ways of trying to develop a relaxed and friendly atmosphere in a group. Firstly, you may need someone to lead the discussion. If there is any doubt that it may be difficult to find someone who is acceptable to the whole group, then a good strategy is to rotate the group leadership. If every group member knows that the responsibility will eventually fall upon them, they may be more tolerant of those doing the job at present.

Secondly, there are techniques which can be used to ensure that a single individual does not dominate the discussion. You can, for example, place a stopclock or similar in the middle of the table. When someone starts to speak they press the stopclock and must stop talking within sixty seconds. This limits what every individual can say. Alternatively, you can have a rule that everyone must at least say something on every topic. This tends to speed up people who speak first because they know many others have yet to speak. It also ensures a democratic involvement in the debate.

Summary

- Engage in academic discussion whenever you have the chance. It is one of the best ways of learning and clarifying your thoughts.
- Try to avoid discussions where people are trying to put forward their own views, rather than exploring an issue.
- Use groundrules to improve the quality and focus of group discussions.

Coping with stress and tiredness

Tiredness is an almost inevitable part of studying, particularly if you are studying part-time. Studying is time-consuming. Even if you are very good at speed reading, studying will always take up substantial amounts of time, and this will make inroads into all your available time. It is not always easy to eliminate activities from your schedule and so the inevitable happens – you stay up later at night to make progress with your studies. This is not necessarily a bad thing, unless you are so tired the next day that you are dysfunctional at work or at your studies. If that happens then the time saved by staying up late the previous night is simply wasted. It is important to observe yourself and your study performance carefully, in order to have sufficient sleep to perform effectively on the following day. If you become too tired then this in itself can induce a feeling of stress, because you feel unable to cope with your course.

Stress can be caused by a variety of other factors too. You may be concerned that the academic standard of your course is too high for you. If you have worries of this type then ask yourself whether you did or did not meet the entry requirements for the course. The answer must be that you did meet them, because otherwise you would not be on the course. Therefore, the course tutor obviously thinks that you are capable of doing the work. So, have a word with one of your tutors about the material you are finding difficult, and usually some kind of help can be arranged.

You may be concerned because you are getting behind with your work. This may be building up a feeling of stress. If this is the case, again it is best to have a word with your tutors. Discuss the problem with them and try to agree a strategy for getting back on schedule. Simply discussing your difficulties will probably alleviate the majority of the stress.

You may feel stressed because you are worrying about your final examinations, or the final assessment of your project or dissertation. This is the most difficult kind of stress to deal with because you cannot really discuss this with your tutors; you have to find a solution yourself. However, there are fortunately several useful strategies you can adopt.

Firstly, think about all of the work you have done during the course. Think of the good grades you have obtained. Think of your academic achievements and you will probably start to feel a little more positive and optimistic about the final assessment.

Secondly, if you know you have planned carefully and systematically for the final exam, then you know you have done all you can. Tell yourself that you have done the best you could, and that there is nothing else you could have done. This may make you feel more positive.

One of the main reasons why people feel stressed in the lead-up to final exams is that they desperately want to achieve the final qualification, yet are worried that something will go wrong right at the end. It is that sense of 'wanting' which is the cause of the stress. The sense of 'wanting success' and of 'wishing for the qualification' causes us stress because we are worried about how we might feel if we fail.

In order to reduce this feeling it is important to focus on our studies now. Try to pick on aspects of your studies which really interest you, and concentrate on your enjoyment of that subject. It is important to gain enjoyment and interest-value from what you are studying, and if you can do that then you will tend to forget the outcomes of your studying.

Alternatively, you can try steady, regular breathing while focusing upon a single concept in your studies. Sometimes going for a short, brisk walk which requires regular, slightly more rapid breathing also helps dispel feelings of anxiety. These are of course, approaching some of the techniques used in meditation. They all share in common the ideal of focusing on the here and now, rather than allowing our minds to drift off into the future and worry us about what might or might not eventually happen. It is when we allow our minds to invent future events that we can easily start to feel anxious and stressed.

Summary

- Don't become so tired that you become dysfunctional.
- If you are concerned about understanding subject matter or the development of the course, then speak to your personal tutor.
- Try to think positively about your studies.
- Develop the habit of enjoying your studies in the here and now, and getting the most out of it today.

Understanding assessment

Assessment is arguably the most important activity in an educational institution because it is on the basis of assessment that academic awards are made. It is crucial that when tutors assess work, they do so against clear and well-understood criteria, and that these criteria are made known to students before they start their work. Unless you know the yardsticks by which your assignment will be judged, it is not always possible to achieve the best focus or approach for your writing.

It is often the case that all assignments for a particular course are expected to comply with certain general criteria. Such general criteria may include aspects such as, all assignments should:

- make reference to relevant empirical studies
- include a bibliography in standard format
- provide evidence to support assertions
- demonstrate caution in making general statements
- avoid bias or stereotyping in the way issues are discussed.

These are the kinds of criteria which can probably be reasonably applied to most academic writing. Nevertheless, there are perhaps a few remaining imprecisions with these criteria. There is no indication of the number of empirical studies which should be mentioned. Different tutors may conceivably hold rather different views. You may be expected to mention three or four in the entire piece of work, or the same number per page. You will also need to know whether you are expected to provide extracts from empirical studies including, for example, samples of data, or whether it will be sufficient to name the author and year of each study in the text. This relates also to the form of the bibliography or list of references at the end of the assignment. You need to know if there is any specified format or whether any reasonably acceptable style is appropriate as long as it is consistent.

Bias and stereotyping refer to a range of possible errors in the way issues are discussed. It is important that you approach a topic under discussion as impartially as possible. The reader should not be able to judge your own particular standpoint from the way you present the topic. It may be legitimate to conclude an assignment with a more personal assessment of the issue, but this should be done in the context of having evaluated both sides of the issue. For example, if you were asked to write an assignment comparing the value of lectures with that of computer-based, self-study materials as a means of learning, you might conclude your assignment as follows:

> The advantages of a lecture are that you know the work is related to your specific course and it is usually presented in a systematic way. Also you can ask your tutor questions at the end or during the lecture. Lectures have the disadvantage that they are only given at specific times; it is sometimes difficult to take down all the notes, and concentration is sometimes difficult. With computer-based learning you can study when it is convenient to you, but the materials are often written for wider, more general use. They may not be so directly related to your course. Also, although interaction is possible with the computer, it is not possible to have the variety of interaction which is possible with a lecturer. Both types of learning are very useful, but if I were to express a personal preference it would still be for the traditional lecture. Although a little outmoded in this high-technology world, a good lecture is still a very efficient means of conveying information.

In this way you can express a personal opinion without standing accused of bias.

Stereotyping involves portraying groups of people as if they always have certain fixed characteristics. One should be very careful, for example, not to use gender stereotypes when refering to particular occupations. For example, it is easy to always refer to senior managers of organisations using the pronoun he, which stereotypes managers as if there was an inevitability about their being men. Not only is this factually incorrect, but it can be read as implying that in some way men are more suitable for management positions. Such stereotyping can help to perpetuate the idea that gender-based patterns of employment are acceptable. Stereotyping should be avoided because it is often factually incorrect, it is unfair, and can help to perpetuate unfair patterns in society.

Quite apart from general criteria, assignments usually have specific assessment criteria which are related to the particular subject matter. Suppose that you have an assignment to complete which involves a small-scale marketing survey to determine people's preferences in relation to a consumer product. Specific criteria for the assignment might be as follows:

- The planning process for the design of the survey is clearly described.
- There is evidence that there is a rationale behind the sample of respondents.
- The data has been summarised using charts and tables as appropriate.
- The results are analysed and conclusions drawn are logical.

When you read criteria such as these for an assignment it is important to give careful attention to them. It is quite possible that marks are being allocated on the basis of these criteria. Even though you may write much more in your assignment and touch on other aspects of the survey, it is important to make sure that you cover these criteria adequately.

The tutor obviously wants to see that the survey has been carefully planned and that this has been documented. It is not enough to plan the survey; you are asked to describe systematically the stages and thought processes gone through. The third criterion makes it clear that you are asked to summarise data wherever possible, rather than simply talking about it.

Similar criteria might occur with one or two other assignments on the course, but they have been written specifically for this assignment because they are seen as being especially relevant. If you are at all uncertain about the meaning of assessment criteria or how to go about meeting them, then it would be very wise to discuss this with your tutor before you start the assignment.

Summary

■ General criteria refer to all assessed work on the course as a whole.

■ Specific criteria refer to a single piece of assessed work.

■ Criteria are used by tutors to arrive at the final mark for an assignment. If you are unsure about the meaning of criteria then it is wise to consult your tutor.

Succeeding at assignments

A useful recipe for success at assignments is to know exactly what you are aiming at and to know that this is what is wanted by your tutors. One way of achieving this is to produce an assignment proposal. This is particularly useful with project work which involves a good deal of planning the work on your own.

The idea of the proposal is to set down exactly what you intend to do for the assignment and then to get your tutor's approval (or otherwise!) for this plan. Assignment proposals are often asked for by tutors, especially for longer projects, dissertations and research studies. They enable the tutor to be sure a student is on the right track, and is not spending too much time on irrelevant work. It is obviously part of a tutor's job to ensure that students have the best advice possible, and the assignment proposal is a useful method for tutors to reassure themselves that students have understood what is expected of them.

From your point of view as a student, however, the assignment proposal is a very good method of ensuring that you are following accurately your tutor's advice. Your proposal should include the following sections:

■ The title of the course; the title and code number (if any) of the particular module you are studying.

■ The specific title you are giving this piece of work or project.

- The aims of the project. These should be expressed in brief sentences, explaining what you hope to achieve by the assignment.
- An explanation of the structure of what you plan to do. If the assignment is an essay, simply give a series of sections which will correspond to a paragraph or group of paragraphs. If the assignment is a project, you can provide the names of the main sub-sections and what they will include.
- A brief summary of any special features of the assignment such as appendices.
- A brief list of the main books or journals which you are consulting.

The proposal should be quite succinct because your tutor will not have very long to read it. When the proposal is complete, send it or give it to your tutor to glance over. It is probably best if you can give it to her (or him) in person, and ask her to look through it straight away. This should be possible if you have kept it to one side of A4 paper. Ask for any comments and whether it looks as if you are on the right track. Tutors are very experienced at reading such proposals quickly, and should be able to give you rapid feedback. You will then have a little advice to help you, coupled with the reassurance that your tutor has seen your proposal.

Most tutors will probably be happy to look at proposals, and indeed many of them may make it a course requirement. The important thing is to keep the proposal fairly brief and to the point. Looking at a proposal is a different matter from looking at a draft of a piece of work. You have not actually started on the assignment proper, and most tutors would probably not feel they were giving you an unfair advantage by offering advice on your proposal. On the contrary, they may probably regard you as demonstrating a sensible approach to your work.

Summary

- Assignment proposals help you to plan your work, and your tutors to feel confident that you know what you are doing.
- Keep the proposal succinct and fairly brief.
- Use the proposal as a working plan for your assignment.

Working by stages

A large part of this book has involved ideas for planning the process of study. However, we should not forget that it is a mistake to make plans and then stick to them too slavishly. This is not to contradict the advice of the previous section, but to amplify it. Study is a developmental and evolutionary process. When we embark on a project or an assignment we cannot always anticipate exactly how it will work out. It is far better to have a plan than no plan at all, but we should not assume that things will develop in exactly the way we predicted.

A common example of this is the collection of data. When we are starting a project we usually make plans to collect a variety of data. If this involves collecting data directly from people then we usually plan the size of the sample and have an idea of who we will ask. The difficulty is that often the people we ask are unable to help us. This often happens at the last minute. Perhaps they do not return the questionnaire; they may be too busy to be interviewed; or they may decide that they do not wish to answer questions on the subject in question. Also it can happen that we plan to survey people at a particular location – e.g. in the college refectory, or at the entrance to a supermarket – but there are simply not enough people there. We may simply have picked the wrong time.

The point to learn from this is that study, like many other activities in life, is very unpredictable. We have to be prepared for the unexpected and then adapt quickly.

We may think that we understand a topic, but when we come to work out some problems we discover that we do not understand it at all. We may plan to borrow a book from the library for a particular assignment, only to discover it is on loan and there are a series of requests for it. Or, we may plan to use a particular software program only to find that we hit a snag or cannot manage an operation with the data which we thought was straightforward.

Studying and learning often demands a rapid response involving the capacity to absorb information and to restructure it in new ways. This restructuring often results in novel patterns of information and new ways of looking at concepts. These new patterns can then be used to help us absorb fresh information, and adapt that too into a pattern of understanding.

The process of using new data and information to construct fresh ways of learning is an example of inductive thinking. Using new conceptual structures to understand the variety of data around us is an example of deductive thinking. Inductive thinking and deductive thinking proceed alternately like two sides of the same coin. Each follows the other in endless cycles of experience and learning. They are arguably the two most important stages of thinking.

When studying we should be aware that the process is incremental. We must be prepared to adopt a flexible approach to assignments. Learning does not always take place in straight lines. Sometimes we move forward, take a pace sidewards, and then forward again. As long as learning continues to take place then we can feel we are making progress.

Summary

- Study plans have sometimes to be modified in the light of the progress of learning.
- Inductive learning involves absorbing new knowledge and transforming it into new conceptual patterns.
- Deductive learning involves using those conceptual patterns to make sense of fresh information.

Revising for exams

Most of this book is directly or indirectly about revising for exams, because in a sense most aspects of study skills relate to the process of revision. From the very beginning of a course it is best to be thinking about consolidating and revising your work as you go along. In a perfect world, there would be no need to revise for exams because you would have learned the work as you went along! Occasionally I have met people who seemed to be able to achieve this. They appeared to be able to concentrate on the work as it was presented, and learn it at the same time.

For most of us lesser mortals, however, we need to revise carefully for examinations. The revision process should start in plenty of time, because there is usually a lot to do! Last minute revision is usually not sufficient to commit large amounts of information to memory. We may also need the time to understand topics which we only appreciated imperfectly when we were first taught them. A well-planned period of revision is not a guarantee of passing exams but it is the next best thing.

The first step when revising for exams is to make certain you know how the examination will be structured and then assessed. If you are doing a formal college course then you can probably rely upon your tutor to provide all of this information. However, you may be an external or private student and not have access to this kind of information and advice.

The definitive information about an examination is always that published by the examinations board or awarding body in the case of national awards, or the relevant university department in the case of degrees. The information is carefully and accurately worded to make sure there are no doubts about how awards are made. Examination regulations are published and circulated to teachers but are also available to be read by students or members of the public. If you are not attached to a school or college then you could ask at your local public library or write directly to the publications department of the relevant examinations board.

As a student the kind of information you should read includes:

- the syllabus
- details of the examinations, including length, number of exams and structure of exams
- past papers and sample papers
- marking schemes
- Chief Examiner's report.

The starting point is the syllabus. You need to be aware of the subject matter which you should know. This is obviously important if you are a private student. If you are studying at a college, your teacher will have been guided by the syllabus, but for all kinds of reasons may have needed to omit certain topics. It is always worthwhile checking through the syllabus to make sure you are revising all that is necessary. In any case it is usually interesting to read through the definitive syllabus.

The syllabus document will also usually include details of the assessment, including the number of examinations, their length, the number of sections and questions, and the number of questions which should be answered. It is essential to brief yourself carefully on all of this information. It may be, for example, that certain sections of the syllabus are covered in the first exam and the remaining sections in the second exam. A careful study of these regulations may suggest strategies for apportioning revision time between different parts of the syllabus. The proportion of the total marks for each examination and for any coursework assessment should also be given.

Sample papers should be studied if possible. They show the type of questions which are typically set, and often incorporate details of the marking scheme, indicating the number of marks allocated for each question and part of question. Past papers are also very useful because they show actual questions which have been asked. Some tutors and students actually go to great lengths to analyse past papers in order to try to predict the questions for the coming examination. To base your entire revision plan on such predictions seems a high-risk strategy. In any case a good essay or examination answer often involves linking together ideas from different parts of the syllabus. If you have been tempted to revise only a very restricted part of the syllabus, you may not be able to demonstrate this capacity to integrate ideas and concepts.

In any particular subject area you may well be able to predict that certain topics will come up in the exam. Most subjects have key topics which are central to an understanding of that subject. It is perfectly reasonable to revise those thoroughly because it is fair to assume that they may be in the examination in some form. However, the real danger is in revising the topic in a single way and then assuming that whatever the question on the topic, you will be able to write down all that you know in the way you have revised it. If you do this you may very well not answer the question, and gain only a poor mark, even though you have memorised a lot of information.

A very useful source of advice is to study the report by the Chief Examiner of the previous year's examination. This will highlight general strengths and weaknesses of responses to different questions, and will enable you and your tutor to eliminate a number of possible errors prior to the examination.

This then is all of the basic information which you need in order to develop your revision strategy. Now there are more practical matters to take into account.

First of all you need to know how to apportion your revision time. You need to know which areas are your strengths and in which areas you need to devote more energy. You may know this simply from your own reflection and understanding, from comments made by your tutor or from your performance in coursework. The other main source of information are the mock exams which often consist of taking a past paper under examination conditions. They should be marked using the standard marking scheme. The results in the mock exams will often give you an idea of your standard, but at the time of the mocks you will probably not have completed all of the syllabus and will therefore be at a disadvantage. Nevertheless they will give you valuable advice on where you should concentrate your efforts.

It is a good idea in the final stages of revision to look carefully at the instructions on past and sample examination papers. Use these instructions to help work out a time management schedule for the exam. Decide how you will divide up your time. Then check with the instructions on the current syllabus, to make sure that you can anticipate the same number and category of questions. Although this can be very useful for planning your time, remember that you should always check carefully in the actual exam, to make sure the instructions have not altered in any way.

Revision is often more effective if you can do lots of practical exercises and not just sit in front of your notes all the time. Try doing a sample question and giving yourself just the amount of time that you would have in an examination. Choose problems or calculations from your exercise books where you know the answer, and try to work them out. Select illustrative problems from textbooks and try to work them out. Also, redraw charts and diagrams without looking at the textbook.

When revising also bear in mind that the sheer number of hours devoted to revision is not necessarily an indication of the amount of material learned. Time spent has to be spent effectively. It is so easy when revising to sit for hours in front of your books, perhaps deluding yourself into thinking that you are learning the material.

A good strategy to try when learning your notes is that of progressive focusing. This is an approach used not only for revision purposes but also by speech-makers and people who need to give presentations or talks in meetings. Start with the longer notes from your lectures, or those you have made from textbooks. As you read them try to condense them into shorter summary notes in another note book. You can retain the same structure for the notes, but simply make them much briefer. The advantage of this approach is also that it gives you a practical activity while revising. You are then less likely to lose concentration.

You can engage in as many rewritings of your notes as you feel appropriate, but each time you should try to reduce the notes still further. Ultimately you should be able to distil them down to a few key words on a postcard or cards. By this time you should have completed all of the understanding of the material, and simply have to refresh your memory by referring to the key words. These should act as prompts for you, reminding you of the background detail to each.

As you get nearer to the exam you therefore have less and less to read. This method also copes with the issue of last-minute cramming. All that remains to be done on the evening before the exam is to check through the key words. If something has slipped from memory then a quick check with the longer notes should put this right. This approach may reduce last-minute tension also, because the key words are a reminder of how much work you have put into the revision process. This may be reassuring and hence reduce any tension.

Revision can be very exhausting, partly because of the concentration required but also because of the fairly repetitive nature of the activity. Try revising in short bursts of say thirty minutes at a time. Then take a ten minute break and do something else. Then back to revision. This may help you to retain more concentration and to achieve more in the same amount of time.

Finally, you need to be wide awake on the day of the examination. Try to get a good night's sleep and you will be better able to cope with any unexpected questions. Staying up very late the night before for last minute cramming is probably not the best strategy. If you must do some last minute memorising then it may be better to go to bed early the evening before and then get up an hour earlier in the morning. Being able to think quickly and clearly in an examination situation is as important in many ways as understanding and memorising information.

Summary

- Check the syllabus and examination regulations.
- Look at sample and past papers and focus on the style and content of questions.
- Consult examiner's reports and put suggestions into practice.
- Plan revision time carefully and adopt a progressive focusing approach.
- Try to build practical exercises into your revision schedule.
- If you tend to lose concentration, try revising in short bursts.

Passing exams

There are many different types of examinations and each has its own requirements. There are specific strategies suitable for a mathematics exam which may be different from those for a business studies exam. First of all though, there are some important general considerations for all examinations.

It is important to read and comply with all of the instructions. It is very easy in the heat of the moment to answer the correct number of questions but not in the correct combination from different sections. The examination invigilator will probably give a brief introduction to some of the instructions concerning filling in your name and course details. In some exams there is a trend to adopt so-called anonymous marking schemes. With this system each candidate is allocated a number which is entered on the script instead of your name. The examiner or marker is then unaware of your identity when marking your script. Your name is only matched with your code number after marking. It is obviously essential to be careful with such systems to ensure your paper can be identified.

You will need to be particularly careful when numbering questions to ensure there is no ambiguity about your answers. Most examination papers which have multiple sections provide advice on the length of time to be devoted to each section. This is very valuable advice and should be carefully heeded. The advised time is usually proportional to the number of marks for each section. It is sensible to do a quick calculation to ensure that you do not exceed a reasonable time for each question and hence fall behind an appropriate schedule.

Different types of examinations pose specific problems. In exams which contain essay questions, it is important to address two important issues with each essay:

- Ensure that you are clear about the concepts used in the title.
- Ensure that you have a planned structure in mind for the essay.

As an example consider the essay title:

To what extent does an educational system influence society? How does society influence its educational system?

This question is phrased in a very general manner. It does not specify a particular country or indeed time in history. On one level it could be a very general, almost philosophical essay. On the other hand, it could be very much about the politics of education in contemporary Britain. Unless there are other clues or instructions, it would be a good idea to map out exactly how you hope to deal with the question. You could, for example, restrict yourself to one country for the purposes of illustration, or you could draw upon a range of countries, both industrially-developed and developing countries.

Secondly, a plan for the essay would be very useful. You could divide the essay into two parts, considering first the effects of education on society, and then the reverse. This would perhaps be the simplest strategy. On the other hand it would be possible to consider both facets in parallel, by looking at general themes such as the economics of education and then, say, the politics of education.

Whichever option you choose, the essay will appear to be much more coherent if you do have a plan rather than just letting the essay evolve. The plan also enables you to manage your time more carefully. You can work out a rough time schedule for when you should be at different stages of your plan.

There is an increasing tendency for colleges to employ multiple-choice questions in examinations. Such examination papers take a long time to plan and set, but once completed they are very easy to mark because the assessment can be computerised using an optical reader. It is particularly important to follow instructions carefully with such exams, particularly in relation to the way you mark your selected response e.g. with a solid line, or perhaps completely shading a small box.

Science exams usually involve calculations of some sort, particularly of experimental results and their interpretation. It is important to show the stages of all calculations and the formulae used, because these indicate to the assessor the thought processes you have gone through. If you happen to make a mistake at some stage in your calculation you will often gain credit for the part you have worked out correctly.

Examinations in many subjects now have data interpretation questions. These involve providing a certain amount of information which, depending upon the subject area, might consist of:

- an extract from a piece of journalism
- some social statistics
- the results of an experiment
- an extract from a novel or a textbook
- graphical or tabular data.

After the data there are a series of questions asking you to interpret the data. The questions do not necessarily involve a lot of writing, but are designed to test understanding and analysis of the data. The critical aspect of such questions is to ensure that you understand the data. It is worth spending enough time to fully analyse the data before you start on the questions.

Summary

- Follow instructions on the examination paper.
- Ensure that you have fully analysed the question title.
- Draw up a basic plan for essays and other questions involving substantial writing.
- Set down all the formulae used and the stages in your calculations.
- In data-response questions, think carefully about the data before you answer questions.

6 ENJOYING YOUR WRITING

Writing for pleasure

Most study involves writing to some extent. Either we are taking notes in a lecture or from a textbook, or we are writing assignments. Of course assignments may not consist entirely of written material. They may involve artefacts such as sculptures, models and drawings, or they may include tape-recordings. However, written work will usually be a major part of them. When you have to produce a piece of writing such as an essay or a project, there is a real danger that this is just seen as a mechanistic task: 'I must produce that essay on time at all costs'. The writing becomes a burden which has to be removed. It can be seen as a necessary evil on the way to a qualification. If we approach writing in this way, then we lose much of the pleasure of the activity.

Obviously assignments must be completed on time and it is important to have a practical approach to this task. Indeed much of this book has been devoted to the development of strategies to complete assignments satisfactorily. However, as with a lot of studying, it is the mental approach to such tasks that matters.

Writing is very much about the pleasure of communicating with others, in this case your tutors. Writing an academic essay is not simply about re-presenting abstract and theoretical ideas from a book. The choices you make of references and of topics to discuss say a great deal about yourself and your view of the world. At the end of an essay it is the norm to summarise the arguments and express a personal viewpoint about the issue. During the essay, it is often appropriate to indicate briefly one or two anecdotes which shed light on a theoretical issue or illustrate a discussion. All of these are ways in which your own voice can come into academic writing and communicate ideas to other people. It is much more creative if this process of communication can be seen as an enjoyable activity rather than merely a pragmatic exercise.

Linked with this is the pleasure gained from receiving a reply. Communication is clearly a two-way process and appreciating the ideas expressed by others is just as important as communicating your own ideas. In the case of assignments the reply is normally the comments by your tutor. These can be seen as simply part of the grading and assessment system, or as a process of communicating ideas. The latter view is in many ways a much more positive view.

Most importantly, writing is a means of clarifying your own ideas. There is something about the very process of committing ideas to paper which requires us to think carefully about the structuring of ideas and how we assemble them. This process is extremely valuable and often leads to a clarification of our ideas. This kind of exploration of ideas seldom takes place in quite the same way in another medium of thought. Certainly just reflecting on something, or even talking about it, does not seem to have the precision of analysis which accompanies the writing process. This process of exploring ideas with the precision of writing is certainly one of the pleasures of writing.

Quite apart from writing assignments there are a variety of ways in which writing can be incorporated into studying and give pleasure at the same time. Here are some ideas.

Get into the habit of writing to friends or relatives describing progress with your studies. Tell them about your lectures, the discussions with fellow students and the topics you are learning about. Describe the books you are reading, and the ideas you are learning about.

If you have read a recently-published book, try writing a book review and send it to a suitable journal. It is best to have a look at one or two journals first in order to examine the typical length and structure of a book review that is appropriate. You could also try telephoning or writing to the reviews editor to check that they are happy to receive unsolicited reviews. Then write one. It can be a very interesting and enjoyable exercise to read a book and then to write a brief analysis of it.

Writing letters to newspapers is a good way to see your writing in print. Newspapers will often publish letters on issues of topical or political interest, and this gives you an opportunity to express your ideas in a systematic way.

If you have a group of friends or fellow students who are interested in the same topics, then you could start a circular newsletter. One person writes a few observations on a subject and passes the newsletter to the next person who adds some further comments, arguments or analysis. The newsletter proceeds until either a new subject develops or the previous subject evolves into a new one. The same effect can be achieved by using email and printing out the responses as they arrive.

Writing a diary or autobiography can be both an enjoyable writing experience and also very useful as a means of learning and reflection. The process of reflecting upon your own life experience and relating this to your studies can be very informative.

Summary

- Concentrate on the pleasures of writing as a process, rather than as merely a means to an end.
- Use writing as a means of exploring your own ideas.
- Write for enjoyment, and try writing letters, circulars and diaries as a way of exploring and communicating your own ideas.

Writing simply and clearly

Some academic writing, written by well-educated academics, can be difficult to understand. This is perfectly reasonable if:

- The ideas are very complex and it is normally expected that you need a preliminary course of some kind before being able to understand them.
- The technical terms used are very specialised and again you need a period of induction into the meaning of the vocabulary.

Most people would accept this. We cannot be experts in everything and it is only to be expected that some kinds of writing will be beyond our comprehension. Equally, it is unreasonable to expect experts to dilute what they are saying by eliminating the correct terms for ideas simply because these terms sound rather complicated. Their subject or discipline may have its own discrete vocabulary and to change that may bring about an unacceptable change in meaning.

On the other hand, it is not reasonable if academic writing is difficult to understand because:

- The ideas are expressed in unnecessarily complex language.
- Complicated language hides a basic lack of structure and logic in the writing.

Academic writing is not difficult to do and should not be difficult to read, if certain very straightforward rules are observed. Here are some simple tips to help you produce clear, accurate academic writing:

- Make sure you have a clear plan of how you intend to present your ideas.
- Write a clear introduction which explains in advance the structure of what you are going to write.
- Have one main idea to each paragraph. The first sentence of the paragraph should introduce the idea.
- Each following sentence should say one thing about the main idea.
- Bring your ideas together in a concluding paragraph.
- Before you write each sentence make sure in your mind you know exactly what you are going to say.
- If you are not sure it is grammatical, read it aloud to yourself. If it sounds right, then it probably is structured correctly.
- Make sure that each word in the sentence is necessary to the meaning, and is the correct word.
- Omit superfluous words.
- Do not use repetitive words. Do not use two similar adjectives if one will do.
- Only use technical words if they are essential to the meaning of the subject. If not, substitute an everyday word with the same meaning.

Some students try to copy the worst kinds of academic writing, and write in a complicated way. This only obscures the message. Jones and Johnson (Vol. 2, 1990) provide excellent advice on writing skills.

Summary

- Academic writing, like all writing, sets out to communicate.
- An idea expressed in straightforward language is more likely to be understood.

■ Only use technical terms if they are an essential part of the subject and cannot be omitted.

Managing without jargon

There is sometimes a temptation to make your writing sound more impressive by using jargon. The latter could perhaps be described as the use of specialised terms out of context. However, some terms are so specialised in their meaning that they could hardly be described as jargon even if someone attempted to use them outside their normal area. Scientific terms are rather like this. It is very difficult to imagine such terms as quantum number or Planck's Constant being used outside the context of theoretical physics. They could therefore not be used as jargon.

Sometimes, however, specialist terms are adopted by people who try to use them in everyday speech. An example is 'existentialist'. Existentialism describes a particular philosophy with a clear academic history and coherent set of ideas within philosophy and philosophical literature. Occasionally you may hear someone say that they 'have taken an existentialist viewpoint' or 'consider something to be an existential experience'. One is never sure whether or not this is an unnecessary use of a technical term. If it is, then it is jargon.

One of the problems with jargon, of course, is that you can easily use a word incorrectly. Existential is such a word. It sounds very impressive, but could easily be misused. There may well be a much simpler word to describe whatever you may wish to say.

Another word frequently read in academic writing is 'phenomenological'. This is a really impressive-sounding word, isn't it! Phenomenology, like existentialism, refers to a particular set of philosophical ideas with an inclusive range of concepts. It represents a complex set of ideas, and the term should only be used in a very precise and careful way, in order to discuss this particular school of thought. Its use in a loose, general sense counts as jargon and is inadvisable, as the writer might be pressed for the exact meaning of what is written. This could prove embarrassing!

Perhaps the clearest forms of jargon involve the use of words which although fairly long, sound as if they have an ordinary, everyday meaning. In fact, they have a very precise academic meaning within a particular subject. If they are used rather casually and unthinkingly in everyday language, then they count as jargon. Here are some examples.

'Socialisation' is a word which has a precise meaning in sociology and yet also finds its way into everyday speech and writing. If the audience understands it then its use is acceptable. If not there are straightforward alternatives. Compare the two sentences:

The child has suffered from inadequate socialisation on the part of family and school.

Family and school could have tried to improve the child's behaviour.

Admittedly there may be subtle distinctions of meaning here as far as a sociologist is concerned, but it is clear that the jargon of socialisation is not absolutely necessary.

In psychology, words such as 'cognition' or 'individual consciousness', can easily be used in the sense of jargon. For example, consider the sentence:

The relationship between individual cognition and the influence of externalities is highly problematic.

This sentence could perhaps be rewritten as:

It is not easy to understand the connection between thought processes and the surrounding world.

Perhaps the two sentences are not exactly synonymous but the second has the advantage of being fairly straightforward and using reasonably ordinary words.

Summary

- Consider the background of your audience when selecting vocabulary.
- Generally try to choose the simplest and most precise words.

Avoiding biased writing

One of the characteristics of academic writing is that it is expected to analyse an issue on purely logical and rational grounds. 'Logical' means that the conclusions drawn should depend purely upon the starting point of the discussion. In other words, the conclusions should not exceed the limits of the initial propositions. If they do, then they are drawing upon information which has not properly been admitted to the discussion.

'Rational' means that reasons should be given for the conclusions drawn. If a discussion starts with an evaluation of some data which has been collected, then it may be possible for the discussion to proceed in different directions depending upon how the data is analysed. The idea of rationality builds in the giving of reasons for taking the discussion in a particular direction. Logic and rationality are thus important cornerstones of academic writing.

One of the main challenges to logic and rationality is the presence of an ideological slant in a piece of writing. Ideology refers to an all-pervading belief system or world view which is the major influence on the way in which a person thinks, writes and conducts his or her life. Perhaps the best known examples of ideologies are some political and religious systems. This does not mean that you cannot be politically-minded without being ideological. You can be extremely interested in politics and yet keep a completely open mind about which is the best political system to adopt. On the other hand, if you have decided that a particular system is the best, and even more than that, this system influences the entire way in which you look at the world, then you are very close to having an ideological viewpoint. It then becomes very difficult, and even impossible, to consider other political systems.

Some political systems may appear to attract an ideological approach more than others, although arguably this rests much more with the individual than the system. You might call yourself a socialist for example, while still accepting that other approaches have an element of virtue in them. On the other hand, you might be a doctrinaire or ideologically-committed socialist who sees no virtue at all in any other system.

To write ideologically is to be biased, and this undermines the value of academic writing. However, there are two strategies which can enable you to write from an ideological point of view and yet rebut the challenge that one is biased.

The first is to admit at the start that one is writing from a particular viewpoint. For example, you might start a project by saying that you are writing it from a Marxist perspective. This means that you intend to use Marxist concepts and ideas, in order to understand and explain the topic. The point about this approach is that it warns the reader from the very beginning what to expect. The reader then is not troubled to find a single perspective used in the writing, because all of the arguments can be set in this context. The reader knows that there are alternative viewpoints.

The other approach is to conclude the writing with a reflective account which shows the ways in which the author's viewpoint has developed. This sets the particular perspective used in the social context of the author's personal development.

However, it should be said that neither of these approaches are perfect solutions to the problem of bias in writing, and arguably if the writer can adopt such solutions then he or she is not writing ideologically anyway. The preferred solution is not to write in a biased way in the first place, and to try to include the full range of viewpoints in what you write.

Summary

- Try to be balanced, fair and objective in what you write.
- If you must write from a particular viewpoint, then make it clear you are adopting this view.
- Try to survey or mention the range of main viewpoints on an issue.

Writing for information and help

One of the great pleasures of being involved in studying and academic life is that people enjoy writing to each other. This is often to exchange ideas, to help each other, to discuss the things they are writing about, or simply to answer an enquiry from an interested colleague or fellow student. The impact of email has greatly extended this facility although there is still a pleasure in receiving communications as paper copy in a traditional way.

You need never be stuck for additional information on a topic, because there is usually someone who can help. There seems to be an unspoken acknowledgement that academic life and study can only continue properly as long as people are willing to share ideas and help each other. Here are some ideas of sources of information. Of course, you need to bear in mind that people are busy and may want to reply promptly but are prevented through pressure of work.

Firstly, there are many groups of writers who actually welcome comments upon their work, or correspondence about it. The authors of academic journal articles usually include an address for correspondence and so communication with them is both invited and straightforward. The address is published normally so that other academics can engage in debate with them about the arguments in their article. However, they probably would not mind responding to questions of clarification from students, as long as very detailed answers were neither asked for nor expected.

Book authors are also generally interested in receiving comments from readers, although communication would need to be through the publisher in most cases. Some authors do, however, publish their addresses in books and actually invite comments upon the book. Generally speaking, authors rely upon sales figures and reviews to provide them with feedback on their work, and direct feedback from readers can be valuable. Many authors would probably not mind helping with information or guidance to a limited degree, although at the same time they would not necessarily feel under an obligation to reply.

Academic conferences are a very useful source of contacts, and this is helped by the fact that conference organisers usually provide a list of names and addresses of conference delegates to each person attending. It is assumed that people do not mind this, as they are usually attending conferences partly to establish contact with people with similar academic interests. People who attend conferences would not find it unusual to be contacted by someone else who was at the conference and is wanting information in relation to the subject of the conference.

Large companies and organisations often provide free of charge a range of information about their products and markets. This is basically marketing information, but can contain useful information if you are a student of business studies, economics, management or accountancy.

Embassies and High Commissions provide useful statistical and tourist information about their countries. Besides these there is a very wide range of local authority and quasi-governmental organisations which produce detailed information about their area. All you really need is a telephone book to get the address and then simply ask for information.

When writing for information, however, there are a few things which it is best to mention. These will help you to obtain the best and most relevant information to your needs. These include:

■ Say who you are; the subject you are studying and where you are a student. This will help to set the context for the recipient. Also mention the name and level of the course you are on.

- State exactly the type of information you want. Be as precise as possible.
- Explain the nature of the assignment. Would you like any illustrations or maps? Do you want to know anything of the history of the organisation?

Remember to say thankyou in advance, and enclose a stamped, self-addressed envelope if you consider this appropriate. In fact, it is sometimes difficult to anticipate how much information may be sent, and some organisations may be quite happy to pay for the postage. Alternatively, you could always offer to refund the postage if required.

Summary

- A wide variety of information and help is available from many organisations simply by asking.
- Be precise about what you want.
- Explain who you are and your studying background, in order for the organisation to know with whom it is corresponding.

Using references

One of the main ways of enhancing a piece of writing is to refer to other authors, whether they be authors of theses, articles, unpublished papers, pamphlets or books. There are many reasons for referring to other works:

- It enables you to show the range of your reading.
- It allows you to demonstrate something of the scope of the field of study you are writing about.
- It enables people who read your work to follow up the subject with what others have written.
- You can back up your arguments by referring to others who have suggested similar things.
- You can illustrate what you write with quotations from other writers.

When choosing writers or books to refer to, it is sensible to choose carefully. You want the work to which you refer to make an improvement in what you have written. You may choose a book for all kinds of reasons, but here are some of the criteria you might choose:

- The writer is well known and an authority on the subject.
- The book is relatively recent. (Sometimes however, an old book is worth referring to because it has become recognised as a key text – a 'seminal' work.)
- It is relevant to your assignment and covers the same kind of arguments.
- The book is stylistically well written and contains many interesting comments which are suitable for quotations.

Many students regard referencing as a very difficult and tedious exercise, which is a pity because it can be rewarding. I have suggested earlier keeping a book or database of suitable quotations and this can eliminate a good deal of the potentially time-consuming work.

The main difficulty experienced by students is remembering how to list all of the main features of the works they have been referring to. Sometimes people get so involved in the system they are using that they become preoccupied with the position and spacing of every comma and semi-colon. This is really to lose sight of the main reason for the full list of details of references, and that is to enable your reader to have sufficient detail so that he or she can identify and locate the original book in a library or through inter-library loan. This is the sufficient condition for a referencing system. If you keep this in mind then you will not be too preoccupied with the details of the process.

It is, however, very desirable that a referencing system is consistent. If a writer keeps swapping and changing how book details are presented, this can be very confusing for the reader.

It is probably easiest to list all the works you have referred to at the end of your assignment. You can entitle this list 'References'. If you also wish to list books which you have consulted as background reading but not mentioned in your assignment, you could list these separately at the back under 'Bibliography'. Both the References and Bibliography entries are listed in the same way, by alphabetical order of the surname of the author. There are three main types of entries, and these are authored books, chapters in edited books, and journal articles. They are entered in the following way:

Authored books

Author surname, initials (Year of publication) Title of book. Place of publication, publisher.

The title of the book is either underlined, or more usually printed in italics. If it is an edited book then the abbreviation (Ed.) is entered after the author initials.

A general example of an authored book entry is:
Smith, J. (1990) *A Book of Study Skills*. Southampton, Skills Publishers.

Chapters in edited books

Chapter author surname, initials (Year of publication) Title of chapter, in Initials and then surname of editor (Ed.) Title of book. Place of publication, publisher.

e.g. Jones, J. (1992) Essay Construction, in J. Smith (Ed.) *A Book of Skills for Writers*. Southampton, Skills Publishers.

In this case also, it is the title of the book which is in italics, and not the chapter title.

Journal articles

Author surname, initials (Year of publication) Title of article, Title of Journal, Volume number, issue number, starting page and finishing page of the article.

e.g. Marks, F. (1991) Assessing the essay, *Journal of Writing Skills*, 18(2) pp.121–143.

These are the main categories of works which are likely to be included in a list of references. From time to time you will want to include a variety of booklets, pamphlets and, for example, government publications. Rather than provide examples of how you could treat many different varieties of publication, I suggest that you apply the above general principles and try to represent the publication as best you can, bearing in mind the principle of consistency.

In the text of your assignment there are several ways of indicating where you have obtained your quotation. The general principle is that you give the surname of the author, the year of publication and the page number on which the quotation can be found in the original. The reader can then use these details to locate the full details of the book in the list of references at the end of the assignment. That information can in turn be used to locate the book in a library.

There are, however, several different ways of referring to works in the text of your assignment depending upon such things as the length of the quotation. For example you might just want to mention a particular author and work as dealing with the kind of topic you are discussing. You can do this in the following way:

> This theory is also widely discussed in the literature on this subject, including Smith (1990, p.71) and Jones (1992, p.33).

Alternatively you may wish to include a very short quotation which can easily fit into one of your normal sentences. You can reference this as follows:

> When discussing the nature of theories, Smith (1990, p.96) argues that a theory 'always exists in equilibrium with practice'.

If you want to use an even longer quotation, it is often better to separate the quotation from the remainder of your writing in some way. You can lead into the quotation by saying, 'Smith (1990, p.26) argues that:'. Then leave an extra line and indent the quotation so that it is clearly separate. You can also put the entire quotation in italics or use narrower spacing than your normal text (or both). The idea is to make it perfectly clear which is your writing and which is the quotation. When the quotation is complete you can also leave an extra line to separate it from the next paragraph of your writing.

There is no clear answer to the question of the number of quotations or references that should be included in a piece of work. The majority of what you write should be your own work. Quotations should not be allowed to dominate what you write, although some subjects lend themselves to extensive referencing of source materials.

If you are unsure exactly how to proceed with a particular piece of referencing then it is a good idea to consult several academic journals. You will probably find an example (or similar example) fairly quickly.

The system of referencing which has been described here is sometimes known as the Harvard System and has become the most widely established system in use in academic writing. An alternative system, used in the past and much less widely used now, involves placing a superscript number in the text wherever a reference is made. The full reference is then provided as a footnote or at the end. This method has its adherents but it is somewhat awkward, particularly if you wish to insert an extra reference. In that case all the subsequent numbers must be increased by one, and it is quite easy to make an error in this. The Harvard System does not suffer from this difficulty.

Summary

- Use references which enhance what you have written, and illustrate your arguments.
- Be consistent in using your referencing system, and try to provide sufficient detail for your reader to locate the original book.

Thinking about your reader

It is easy to think of assignments as simply being written for your tutor. It is true, of course, that the lecturer who teaches a module and who sets the assignment will also normally be the person who marks your work. However, it is often the case that assignments are often double-marked or moderated by another tutor. Finally, there is the external examiner for the course who will also read a sample of work.

The point about this is that it is very tempting for a student to try to write for their lecturer, saying the kind of things it is assumed the tutor will approve of, and trying in some cases to reiterate the exact arguments developed in lectures. Some students may say that such a strategy is only prudent and is an attempt to maximise the chances of passing the assignment. Well it may be based on an understandable strategy and it is possible to sympathise with the approach, but such a plan is unlikely to produce work which will attain a high grade. The lecturer will not be very interested in reading his or her lectures rephrased and reworked by a whole class of students. Certainly other tutors and the external examiner will find the work very repetitive. The lecturer will probably take this approach as being evidence of a lack of wide reading and of an inability to create new ideas.

The worst result of such a strategy, however, is that it reduces the act of writing to mere repetition, rewording and a very dependent approach on the ideas of others. With this approach writing can scarcely be a pleasure, but becomes a functional task designed purely to pass an assignment with the minimum of effort. Writing should be much more than this:

- It should be creative and combine the ideas of others in new and novel ways, adding your own ideas to produce an interesting synthesis.

- It should be an exploration of human ideas and thought which does not merely use the recommended source materials of the tutor, but searches for new ideas, new writing and new stimuli to extend the scope of what is written.

- It should be a conscious act of communication; a question of having something you want to say. Writing should stem from a strong interest in something, even a passion for it. If you are really interested in a subject, then this will be conveyed in your writing. You will not be able to avoid it.

- It should be enjoyable, involving the combination of words to express your ideas in the best possible way. Using the most appropriate words in the best combinations is akin to the painter mixing colours on the palette to create just the right hue. There is a pleasure in combining and mixing words in this way.

Writing is all of these things and they should be celebrated even when producing assignments whose main purpose admittedly is to help a student pass a course. Your assignments will be infinitely better if you try to be innovative in combining ideas; if you draw on a wide and interesting range of sources; if you think carefully about the issue at hand and take a well considered stance; and if you then take enjoyment in transmitting that viewpoint.

It is possible to use the actual act of writing as a means of developing ideas. You rely on the process to help your ideas evolve. However, this may not always result in prose which is easy to follow. It is better to think out clearly in advance what you wish to say and then to write it down. In that way, you will present your ideas more clearly to the reader.

The paradox of thinking about the creative aspect of writing is that you will create writing which is far more enjoyable and interesting for your reader. Of course, if your tutor has given you certain structural requirements for the assignment which you should meet, then you must comply, but there is usually a great deal of leeway left to explore the kind of principles outlined above. By following these you are thinking about your reader and creating the kind of writing which he or she will want to read. You should also find that you are enjoying the process much more yourself.

Summary

■ Think about your reader by producing interesting, stimulating prose.

■ Develop new combinations of ideas which are thought-provoking.

■ Think of important things which you want to say to your reader, and then say them.

Using abbreviations and acronyms

It can be frustrating to have to keep writing out a lengthy name in an assignment and it is usually preferable for the writer to use an acronym or abbreviation. An acronym consists of the initial letters of the words in a name, and many acronyms are so common that they have effectively replaced the full version of the name. In fact, people will often be hard-pressed to work out the full version of the name. The acronym has become, through very common usage, the de facto name. Abbreviations simply consist of shortening a long name in some way.

Both abbreviations and acronyms share several potential drawbacks when you are using them in assignments, such as:

■ People may use the same abbreviation to stand for two or more different names, e.g. OUP could be Oxford University Press or Open University Press.

■ Used extensively acronyms can break up prose and make it very awkward to read.

■ Where several different acronyms are used it is easy to forget what each stands for.

■ Acronyms and abbreviations also do not sound very comfortable to read when they occur at either the beginning or end of a sentence.

Whether you invent your own abbreviation for a term or use one which is well established, it is important to use it in conjunction with the full name on the first occasion it is employed. Write the name or term in full and then place the abbreviation in parentheses immediately afterwards. From then on you are entitled to use the acronym on all occasions. At the front of the assignment there should also be a list explaining the abbreviations used in the piece of work. This enables the reader to check up on a meaning if it has been forgotten.

The use of full stops and capital letters can often be confusing with abbreviations. In the case of acronyms it is normally unnecessary to use full stops after each letter. So, for example, it is usually better to write BBC and ITN rather than B.B.C. and I.T.N. Abbreviations such as Ph.D. usually carry full stops. The use of full stops in expressing currencies can be confusing. The use of p to express pence does not normally carry a full stop whereas the letter F. (with full stop) is used after the numerical amount for French Francs.

If you select your own abbreviation because, for example, there is no standard form, you may need to use capitals throughout your assignment. For example, if using an abbreviation for a fictional Northern City Bank you could write:

The Northern City Bank (henceforth referred to as the Bank) ...

You would always use an initial capital letter for Bank because it refers to a specific bank and not to banks in general.

Summary

- Use acronyms and abbreviations to avoid tedious repetition of terms.
- Make sure that there is no ambiguity in their use.

7 | DEVELOPING YOUR LEARNING SKILLS

Using computing for learning

Computers have revolutionised education, so much so that it is difficult to keep up with even a fraction of the developments in software and the Internet. However, even at a basic level it is easy to enlist the help of computers to assist you with your studying.

You no longer need to keep all your study notes as paper copy. You can try transfering key aspects of your notes and assignments to computer disc. One advantage of this process is that it encourages you to organise your work systematically. Each topic should really be saved as a different file with a separate file name. The very act of doing this encourages you to title and classify your information in order to save it. Of course two people will probably not classify the same information in the same way, but the process itself is very helpful. You will need to keep a key of file names either in a notebook or on a hard disc so that you will be able to identify a particular file simply from the code name. It is also a good idea to type a footer in very small print at the bottom of each page. When printed out this identifies and links the paper copy with the file name. Simply from a sheet of printout you can then immediately identify the correct file.

Computers enable you to take full advantage of modern presentational techniques with your assignments. Desk-top publishing packages enable decorative effects to be achieved with assignment cover sheets and with borders and text. Care should be taken, however, with an excess of such decoration in academic assignments. Tutors prefer to concentrate on the content of assignments and not on rather superficial aspects such as an ornate cover. A little embellishment is no bad thing, as long as there is a proper concentration on academic content.

There are a number of straightforward things which can make the appearance of assignments look very professional, indeed like pages from a printed book. Quotations can be printed in italics and indented from the left-hand margin. This makes them stand out from the rest of the text. If the right-hand margin is also justified like the left, then the pages of your assignments will look more professional. The use of bullet points is another simple technique which gives a much better presentation to lists of names or topics.

The use of the word-count facility enables you to check at each stage of an assignment whether you are on target to write the correct number of words. Most computers have a very simple facility to enable you to draw tables or histograms. These are a convenient way of summarising numerical information and are very easy to draw on the computer. Their main advantage is that they enable you to summarise information in an attractive and easily readable form instead of having to write a lot of descriptive prose.

A most useful way of using a computer to help you with studying is to keep an academic curriculum vitae (c.v.) which you can add to and expand when necessary. A c.v. is extremely useful when applying for new courses or for jobs, but it is also a very good idea as a means of recording your achievements. The best way is to open a new file on a disc and then entitle it Curriculum Vitae (or a suitable abbreviation). You need then to enter a number of subheadings which might be as follows:

> Name
> Current position
> Educational background
> Qualifications
> Employment record
> Academic interests
> Publications

You can use whatever subheadings you wish, and some of them may need subdividing further. For example, under Educational background you can list schools which you attended and then college or university. You could have a separate sub-section for posts of responsibility you held at schools, and societies which you joined. Be sure you mention any achievements such as a prize at speech day. Under Employment record you can mention part-time jobs, particularly noting any responsibility you held. Under Publications you could mention such things as an article or poem in a school magazine, or a letter published in your local newspaper.

You should think of your c.v. not as a brief list of items, but as a detailed life record which lists all of your achievements, adding all of the details where relevant. The great advantage of having your c.v. on a disc is that you can update it all the time, printing off a new version whenever necessary. Hudson et al. (1997) contains valuable information on using computers in learning.

Summary

- Keep your notes in sections on a computer disc.
- Upgrade the presentation of your assignments using desk-top publishing.
- Prepare your c.v. on computer disc and update it regularly.

Using libraries

Most people have their own particular ways of using libraries. Some are browsers who stroll between the shelves and hope to find a useful or interesting book. Others use a very scientific approach, looking up a subject or author in the computerised catalogue and then trying to locate the relevant article or book. In addition, the nature of libraries is changing as they employ a wider range of reference materials. Libraries are using more non-book materials such a video and audio-tapes, and computerised materials. This is what some of the students surveyed said about their techniques for using libraries when preparing for work on an assignment:

> 'I read the relevant texts or find video and audio support and then make notes. I formulate my own views then and write what I believe to be relevant.'

> 'I read wide and varied excerpts from relevant literature and previous seminar notes, in order to find suitable material.'

> 'I try to find the relevant literature, having defined the subject area.'

> 'I research the subject e.g. look it up in the library and do the background reading; once I've picked out the relevant points I try to compose them into an essay.'
>
> 'I look at apparently relevant books in the library, and select ones which look as if they are helpful.'
>
> 'I find relevant texts including books and journals, and write an essay plan, finding quotes to back it up.'

All of these quotations make especial mention of the notion of relevance, and perhaps this is the fault of tutors who publish reading lists and ask students to locate specific books. It is easy to give the impression that only certain books and articles are relevant. It is perhaps worth looking at this issue of what is relevant.

If your tutor recommends certain books or articles on a reading list then this can save you a lot of time in a library. You can look up the book in a catalogue and go straight to it. You know it is going to be suitable for the assignment and at about the right academic level. However, it is worth remembering that tutors cannot list every suitable book. There will almost certainly be many others which are not on the list. Also, if all students go for the same few books, not only will all the assignments be very similar but the copies of the books will soon disappear from the library shelves. Everyone will be attempting to borrow the same books.

Searching out alternative sources is not always too difficult. Start with other books by the authors of the recommended texts. Have a look at the bibliographies in the recommended texts. These will direct you to the books consulted by that author.

Other strategies include looking in the same sections in the library as the recommended texts; looking at journals with suitable connected titles for articles; and finally (and rather more scientifically) looking at the various collections of abstracts of articles which are in paper copy or on CD-ROM or computer. An abstract is a summary of a journal article which explains concisely the methodology and the results and gives the exact details of how to locate the article. Even having decided on the articles you want, however, there is still the problem of locating the journal and also the exact volume and issue number which you want. This is not always straightforward. Very often the quickest way of locating suitable additional reference material is to use the library indexing system to identify half a dozen journals which publish in the subject area you want. If you look at, say, the issues of the last two years, you would be a little unlucky not to find something of interest. It may not be exactly what you wanted, but it may be connected in some way. At the very least this method is quick and also rapidly widens your awareness of the subject area.

Summary

- Take full advantage of the wide range of non-book materials in libraries.
- Don't rely exclusively on tutor reading lists. Explore the literature yourself.
- Make use of the indexes of article abstracts.

Memorising coursework

Many students tend to put off learning coursework until they are revising for exams, and yet this is a very inefficient method of learning. Considerable amounts of factual information accumulate and become difficult to memorise in a short space of time. It is much better if you can learn course material as you proceed through the course.

Generally we find that we often remember things without really trying. Some things just tend to stick in our minds. This usually happens though because we have a particular interest in the topic. We remember the actors and actresses in a film because we really liked that film. We remember the scores of tennis matches because we like to play tennis ourselves. We remember the words of a song because we love the words and the music, and perhaps they have some special association for us. Our memory works so effectively in these cases because there is a strong connection between ourselves, our own interests, and the subject matter we are remembering. In other words, there is significance for us in the topic we are remembering.

Using the concept mentioned in Chapter 1, the subject matter being remembered has associations with Real People. One reason why we do not find it as easy to remember chemical formulae, Latin verbs, and mathematical equations is that they do not on the face of it have connections with Real People. They seem abstract ideas which we only need to learn for examinations. Memorising them does not come easily to us because firstly, they seem devoid of any personal relevance and secondly, we feel we have to learn them for exams. There is a sense of compulsion and at the same time a feeling of reluctance. We remember things most easily when we want to remember them because they seem interesting to us.

One of the things which most good teachers try to do all the time is to point out to their students the relevance of the subject matter. This may seem relevant to their own lives, or relevant in a wider context of an important group of people or to the world at large. It is this relevance which helps to motivate people to study and also to memorise things.

When trying to memorise chemical formulae, Latin verbs, or mathematical equations, one strategy is to use the Real People Approach to think of ways in which the topics to be memorised can be significant for you or for others. If you are studying chemistry then you will probably be able to think of uses for the particular chemicals. Think of how they are manufactured; by whom; how and where they are used and by whom. This will 'bring the chemical formula to life'. It will no longer simply be a collection of symbols for atoms joined by different sorts of chemical bonds.

Mathematical equations may be rather more difficult to use to generate a Real People Approach, but it can be easier with applied mathematics, statistics and probability than with pure mathematics. In the former cases problems are usually contextualised in readily understandable practical situations. You can easily relate mathematical equations to problems associated with bridge building or launching space rockets. In pure mathematics it is necessary to think generally about the use of mathematics whether it is in finance or accountancy, or in, say, conducting a census of the population.

Finally, Latin verbs may not seem very relevant to everyday life, until we consult an etymological dictionary and realise the number of 'English' words which are derived from Latin. We then discover that in a sense we are 'speaking' Latin ourselves. Latin then becomes much more significant, quite apart from the value of learning about Roman history and culture.

Summary

- Explore your own memory and try to work out why you remember some things and not others.
- When learning topics for tests or exams, always try to work out ways in which you can use the Real People Approach; this should help you memorise them.

Becoming analytic and critical

One of the most important qualities of the student is the ability to think and write clearly. In attempting to do this there are a few key questions which if asked regularly will help you to think precisely, not only about what you read but also about what you write. Such questions include:

- What is the central feature of the writer's argument?
- Is there sufficient evidence to justify the conclusions drawn?
- Do some of the words used have different meanings in different contexts?

It is important when reading a passage to be able to ignore the relatively superficial material and identify the core argument. Only when you have done this are you able to decide whether there is sufficient evidence to support the argument. Different writers employ many kinds of evidence. One of the most common in academic writing is the argument from authority.

Someone will make an assertion that a particular government policy, for example, was totally ineffectual and will mention in parenthesis a writer who supports this view. The reader is invited to assume that because someone else takes the same view, that this strengthens the claim substantially, or perhaps the reader is invited to assume that this makes the argument true. One never quite knows what the writer is saying or suggesting to the reader. All we know is that the referenced writer is there to support the writer's claim. The more famous or celebrated the referenced writer, then presumably the more the writer thinks that the original claim is supported. The quoted writer is there because there is an assumption that they are an authority on the subject. Sometimes an argument from authority is put even more explicitly. An academic authority is quoted as in the sentence: 'The leading Professor of Geophysics and Nobel Laureate, argues strongly that ...'.

We are invited to believe that because of the individual's credentials and reputation, they have certain insights and wisdom which we should accept. One of the strengths of the argument from authority is that we clearly have to rely on academic authority for all kinds of decisions – many of which we are unable to challenge. If an astronomer appears on the evening news and says she has discovered a new galaxy many light years away, we accept this as true because we are in no position to challenge her expertise. On the other hand, if another eminent astronomer suggests that meteorite showers have been responsible for a dramatic increase in the potholes on our motorways, we should at least pause and think. This is an area in which we could form our own opinion about the expert's analysis. Have we seen any meteors recently? Could the potholes have been caused by other factors? What evidence can the famous astronomer adduce for this claim?

In many cases of arguments from authority the nature of the evidence is so specialised that we are unable to evaluate it, and must take the specialist's judgement on trust. In other cases, however, the specialist's judgement impinges upon our everyday experience and we actually are in a position to evaluate it.

In other cases, experts are not always in agreement, and although we may not understand the most sophisticated aspects of their arguments, we can still form a judgement about which argument we prefer. Economic and political arguments are frequently of this type. We may not necessarily understand all of the complexities of fiscal policy decisions, but we often can form an intuitive judgement based on the effects which we assume a particular economic policy will have on ordinary people.

Yet again, specialists will sometimes argue that a particular line of action is best, or that people ought to behave in a certain way. These are evaluative judgements and we can often form an opinion about such ethical pronouncements. We recognise that what is supposedly good for one person may not be good for another. Words such as 'should', 'ought', 'right', 'fair' and 'just' have very different meanings for different people. Even on the lips of a specialist in a particular subject, such ethical judgements may not have wide appeal.

When both reading and writing academic prose we should be careful when employing the work and words of others to support our own arguments. We need to ask ourselves why we are using the work of others to add to our arguments. Is it because:

- We hope to make truth claims based upon the support of others?
- We hope to strengthen our case?
- We hope to show that at least one other person thinks the same as we do?
- We want to give an example or illustration of another viewpoint?
- We are clear about what we want to achieve (then hopefully our readers will be also)?

Summary

- When reading or writing ask yourself:
- What is the key argument being advanced?
- What is the purpose of refering to others in this argument?
- What evidence is brought to bear to support the argument?
- Is the evidence relevant and valid?

Presenting your work

The main rule when presenting your assignment is to consider the convenience of the person who will read it. Of course, you also want the satisfaction which comes from presenting your work neatly and attractively. However, the main consideration must be that it meets the needs of your reader or the tutor who is to assess it.

Always make sure that you include basic, relevant information on the front of the assignment, including the title of your essay or project and your name. If appropriate, state the course on which you are enrolled and the name of your tutor. You may also want to record the date of submission, and the name and code number of the module for which the work is submitted. As you prepare the front sheet, ask yourself whether the assignment were misplaced or ended up in the wrong location, would there be enough information for the finder to send it to the correct place.

Sometimes tutors ask for assignments to be packaged in a particular way. If not, then it is worth thinking about how you will package your work. It is not a good idea, for example, to present a 3,000 word assignment in a ring binder. There will be so much spare room that the assignment will flap about and may even be torn from the hole punch binding. In any case your tutor will not want to carry around twenty ring binders. Much better to use a stiff plastic folder which fits the assignment snugly. It will be lighter and easier to carry and will actually be better protection. Remember, though, that it is better to have a wide margin on the left-hand side of the paper of your work, as width is lost in the binding – otherwise it is difficult to read the text.

Page numbering is important. It makes your work look professional, and when your tutor writes a commentary on your assignment it is much easier if reference can be made to a specific page. Some students add headers and footers on every page in very small text, detailing such features as their name and the title of the assignment. This kind of detail may be appropriate in a journal, but it can rather detract from the content in a student assignment.

A good contents page is always a useful addition to an assignment. It should indicate the main sections and refer to the correct page numbers. The contents page is a great help to the reader of an assignment. It indicates the main sections which can be expected, and allows the reader to become oriented to the main sequence of argument of the assignment. The division into suitable sections also makes the assignment easier to read, as the information is presented in more easily absorbed units.

Footnotes, especially involving the use of superscript numbers in the text, are less commonly seen nowadays, and probably best avoided. If there are things which you want to add to the text and they really cannot be placed in the text, then they should come under a Notes section immediately prior to the references. Appendices, as a general rule, should be kept to a minimum. There are usually no extra marks for lots of appendices. They can even be an irritant for the marker who regards them as an unnecessary and bulky addition to the main text.

Finally, always keep a copy of your work, including any original documents submitted as appendices. If you are a part-time student and want your work posting back to you, then add your postal address at the end of the assignment.

Summary

- Think of the needs of the assessor when presenting your work.
- Choose a binding which is slim, secure and protective; preferably with a transparent plastic front cover.

■ Consider dividing your work into sections; have a clear contents page and number all pages.

■ Leave an extra wide left-hand margin for binding.

Learning study vocabulary

Academic writing tends to employ particular kinds of words irrespective, to some extent, of the particular subject. The fundamental reason for this is the nature of the academic process. One theme mentioned throughout this book is that academic writing tends to avoid claims of certainty about things. This is a feature of the scientific paradigm within which most academic writing occurs.

Discussion is a word which is commonly used in this respect. It is a useful word to use in the title to an assignment. For example, you might use the following as an example of a title: 'A discussion of the issues affecting the expansion of space exploration in the 1960s'. The use of the word discussion implies here a sense of working towards the truth. It suggests that while the main issues are perhaps known, there is some slight uncertainty in the relationship between them and their causes.

I have just used in the last sentence another word which is very valuable in academic writing and that is 'perhaps'. It is used for the precise reason mentioned in the last paragraph. Other similar words and phrases are 'normally', 'generally', 'apparently', and 'in the majority of cases'. All of these words and phrases give a sense of the provisional nature of scientific enquiry.

It is often necessary in assignments to talk about the general direction from which you are approaching a problem. Alternatively you may want to speak of the general range of concepts and ideas being used to analyse a problem. Here the word perspective is very useful. You can speak of approaching a problem from a particular perspective; or of addressing an issue within a particular perspective or framework.

When analysing an issue it is often necessary to start that analysis at a particular point. You cannot always go back to the most basic or fundamental starting points. You have to, in other words, make certain assumptions. The latter form the conceptual starting point for your enquiry, and so you might say: 'This enquiry starts by making the following assumptions ...'.

Much academic enquiry involves the process of comparison. Experimental procedures are compared; sample populations are compared; and statistical techniques are compared. It is always preferable having made a comparison, however, to say that 'comparisons suggest that …' rather than 'comparisons prove that …'. 'Proof' is always a word which it is best to avoid, since it suggests a finality to the process of enquiry which is rarely justified.

When you are collecting information a useful descriptive word to use is 'data'. The word 'information' does sound a rather everyday, non-technical term which is used in all kinds of non-academic contexts. The word data, however, is sufficiently general to be used in a variety of subjects and also to describe data which is both qualitative and quantitative. From time to time, students are tempted to refer to collecting data as the collection of 'facts', and this is really inappropriate. It again carries the same implication as the word 'proof' – a sense of finality.

When the word data is being used there is a question of whether it is singular or plural. Technically the singular word is datum, signifying a single piece of information; while data is the plural form. However data does often tend to be used as a collective noun and hence can be treated as singular for grammatical purposes.

When data is being treated systematically in order to work out what can be induced in general terms, then it is common to say that the data is being analysed, and then interpretations are being made on the basis of the analysis. The word interpretation again implies that there is no finality about what is said. It suggests that other individuals may have drawn a different interpretation.

Summary

- Academic writing tends to have its own characteristic vocabulary, which emphasises the provisional nature of the scientific approach.
- Avoid words such as 'proof' and 'facts', which suggest absolute certainty.

8 CONSIDERING YOUR LONG-TERM PLANS

Building on achievements

One of the most significant changes in our further and higher education systems in recent years has been the development of credit accumulation and transfer systems. Previously it was usually necessary to complete a whole course before you gained recognition for your work. That final recognition usually depended upon a major assessment, such as final exams right at the end of the course. The major change has been to give incremental credit for pieces of work on courses, and this has literally meant that you can build upon your achievements.

As you complete and pass units and modules you accumulate the academic credit and know exactly how near you are to completing your award. This brings a sense of achievement and can create motivation as you get feedback from results. There have been a number of consequences for students from these changes, which have meant that there is much more flexibility in academic systems.

One suggestion is that you should think creatively about the combination of modules you want to study on your course. Gone are the days when you had to stick strictly to a single subject programme. Try to think of the combination of modules which will best suit your future study plans or your future career needs, and ask about them. It is usually possible to set up an individualised programme for yourself, but you often have to ask tutors and make some of the arrangements yourself. Wherever you are studying there will almost certainly be a book or books, containing lists of available modules and a description of the curriculum content. You will also need to take advice on any modules which may need certain prerequisites in order to study them. For example, advanced mathematics modules may require you to have studied more basic ones first.

Some of the modules you want may not be taught in the same department as your main course. This is not necessarily a problem. You may need to join an existing class and special arrangements needed to transfer the credit to your home department. These things are, however, perfectly possible to arrange.

Some courses have so-called staged awards. This means that when you have gained a certain number of credits you can leave your main course, if you wish, with the staged or intermediate award. The main effect of this arrangement is that you can have a break in your studies and yet still have the satisfaction of knowing you have gained an award. When you are ready to resume your studies, you can then carry on and gain the final award.

You need also to think about future courses you might do. One effect of credit accumulation schemes has been that institutions have increased considerably the variety of courses they offer. These often consist of new combinations of existing modules with perhaps just a few new modules added. You need to think carefully about the particular course which will suit you, and again what that might lead on to.

Courses have become more varied in their content and the way they are delivered. Many of them incorporate periods of practical experience in industry and you receive credit for the report and analysis you write of your placement. Qualifications at all levels are changing and adapting. It is now possible to incorporate a taught element for which you gain credit in a doctorate programme. Such changes are revolutionising learning because they are opening up far more opportunities, particularly for part-time students.

Summary

- Credit accumulation systems have increased the number and flexibility of courses.
- Consider trying to combine modules to create the kind of course you want.
- The increase in the number of courses means that you need to do more personal market research before deciding which programme is most suited to your needs.

Linking study to a career

For many people, even those following a formal course, study is an end in itself. It is enough to be studying an interesting subject and to enjoy the reading and the mastery of new knowledge. This is possibly the form of study which is the most motivating in the sense that the sheer enjoyment of acquiring new knowledge and understanding drives us on to do more and yet more study. Many of you, no doubt, study at home in this precise sense. Others find that the additional extrinsic motivation of working towards a qualification helps to sustain interest and a sense of direction.

For many people though, study is very much connected with the idea of getting a job, or perhaps getting a better job. In that sense study is a vocational activity. Most study is vocational, of course, not merely subjects such as accountancy, dentistry, secretarial studies or hairdressing. Study as an activity tends to develop the kinds of skills that are sought-after employment skills such as good written communication, oral communication, the capacity for logical thought, and the ability to absorb and analyse information. Having said this, however, there is a tendency for employers to want future employees who have many of the skills and much of the knowledge to make a useful contribution from the very beginning. If a new employee is economically useful from the first day of employment, then it costs the company much less in on-the-job training and development.

This has led many courses to combine subjects and disciplines in what may at first seem unusual combinations, but which are specifically tailored to the needs of particular jobs. Some courses are even linked to large employers nearby, and train students very specifically for jobs in that company. An example of a combined subject course might be engineering with communications, for people who wanted to work in marketing and sales work for an engineering company; or, law with a modern European language for those who want to work with the legal aspects of the European Union.

Another important way in which study is linked with a career is through the work placements mentioned in the previous section. It is important when embarking on a course which involves a work placement, to check on the kind of placements which are available. You want to make sure that the placement is with the type of organisation for whom you would like to work when you finish your course. It is often the case that employers use the work placement system to assess the performance of possible future employees. It is one of the best possible ways to obtain a foothold on a future career, while for the employer it is an opportunity to judge your abilities.

A major change which has come hand in hand with credit accumulation systems is the awarding of academic credit for experience in the workplace. The argument here is that many of the skills and knowledge gained in the workplace are equivalent to what is taught on formal courses. This is particularly the case when so many courses these days combine academic modules with modules which are much more closely connected with a vocation. For example, there may be a straightforward parallel between a module on accounting and the experience of someone who prepares company accounts.

The best strategy here is that when you are embarking on a course, think of your own work experience and how it might relate to any of the modules on the course. If you think there is a connection, then ask the course tutor if you can have any credit for your experience. You may find you are asked to produce evidence of your experience so that your tutor can decide whether you have met the requirements of the module. You may need to produce references from a past employer saying that you have certain skills, or examples of documents you have written which show your knowledge in a particular area. You may even be asked to sit a short examination or practical test.

The acceptance of prior learning within the world of education has been an important step in the recognition of workplace learning as being in some cases equivalent to academic learning. You should consider applying for recognition of prior learning as it may save you study time and possibly some course fees.

Summary

- Consider trying to combine modules in ways which will help you apply for a job or start the career you want.
- Choose your work placement carefully in order to maximise your chances of getting into your choice of career.
- Consider applying for accreditation of prior learning as a way of gaining credit for your previous employment experience.

Planning for a lifetime of learning

There has traditionally been the feeling that it was possible to train for a job or undertake a course of study while fairly young, and that this would last for one's working life. Education was seen as a once and for all event which equipped one for life. This kind of attitude was perhaps sustainable in a world which changed relatively slowly and in which one could be fairly certain of a job for life, and even of the same job for life. However, this is no longer the world in which we live. There is likely to be the need to train and then to retrain perhaps several times in one's working life. These economic and employment factors have been instrumental in changing our attitudes to lifelong learning.

This is what some of the students surveyed said about lifelong learning:

'Having completed many years of part-time study I feel that it is an ongoing process which is part of my life, and helps me in a rapidly-changing work environment.'

'I believe lifelong learning is important for personal enrichment and also to be employable.'

'Lifelong learning is a very important principle to me personally, but I am not sure whether this is a general feeling in society. Whether or not you go in for lifelong learning is a personal thing.'

'Lifelong learning is becoming more important because technological change is much more rapid these days. You need to keep learning in order to keep up to date with developments.'

There are two main aspects of lifelong learning which emerge from these interesting quotations. One is that lifelong learning is about personal enrichment. The principle of learning is one which is linked to having an enquiring attitude towards the world. There is a sense of being curious, of wanting to master new skills for their own sake and of wanting to extend one's knowledge and understanding. Many people see these as worthy goals which make for a more interesting and worthwhile life.

On the other hand there is the concept of lifelong learning as being a pragmatic approach to re-skilling or professional updating. In many areas of professional activity, notably Information Technology, it is necessary to update continually and become familiar with the latest developments. Professional updating and retraining are however, as much a state of mind as they are, practical initiatives. It can be argued that the best approach to lifelong learning in this respect is to be updating continually whether or not there appears to be an external reason or justification. If you wait until you need to retrain, then arguably you have left it rather late. Here are some simple ideas for lifelong learning in terms of professional updating. They are easy to implement and can have a dramatic effect out of all proportion to the relatively small effort needed to carry them out:

- Subscribe to a relevant professional journal (or read it in the library).
- Read job adverts in your area, not necessarily with a view to applying, but to stay up to date with the skills and qualifications which are being asked for.
- If you are in employment, make it known that you are interested in attending updating courses.
- Watch out for adverts detailing academic conferences and try to attend. These are not all prohibitively expensive.
- Look at adverts for courses, and also college and university prospectuses. These are normally free and readily available. You can build up your own reference collection and make yourself familiar with entry requirements and the extent of accreditation of prior learning which is offered.

Learning and the pursuit of skills and knowledge is one of the main ways in which human beings create a sense of meaning in their lives. To seek to understand the world better is probably one of the deepest-seated instincts in people, and the concept of lifelong learning exemplifies this.

Summary

- Treat life as a journey in search of knowledge and wisdom.
- Use learning to create a sense of meaning and to help you fulfil your career aspirations.
- Develop your personal action plan for lifelong learning.

Setting up a learning group

Making contact with people who have similar academic interests and getting to know them well is not something which happens quickly. You have to work at it and slowly develop the contacts. Very often your learning group will develop from simply one contact between two people. If they find this works then this single contact will lead on to others. Their contacts will meet or communicate with each other, and they in their turn will introduce new people. Before long a true learning network has been established.

The author knows of one such network which developed from an accidental meeting on an airline flight between two college teachers from different countries. Having discovered that they shared certain professional interests they agreed to write and to look into the possibility of staff exchanges. Even though they each taught in rather different institutions, it quickly became apparent that their colleagues would benefit greatly from meeting each other. Exchanges followed and over a considerable length of time two colleges geographically and culturally quite far apart, were linked, and the staff shared a very useful and constructive learning group.

Learning groups do not come together by accident. It is often necessary to work hard at setting them up. Moreover, it is necessary to cultivate that open approach and frame of mind which is conducive to taking advantage of opportunities when they present themselves. One has often got to recognise an opportunity as such and to take advantage of it. The opportunity may just be a chance meeting or an introduction brought about by a third party. Nevertheless, even the briefest of meetings can be used as the basis of setting up a more permanent group.

On other occasions it is sometimes possible to create a learning group quickly by using a group of students or colleagues, who have come together for a different but specific purpose. If all the members of a class exchange addresses and telephone numbers and academic interests, then they will be able to communicate and set up small groups with similar interests. It is not sufficient, however, simply to be in contact with people of similar interests. What is important is to have a clear idea of why you are communicating and what you are seeking to achieve.

When you are developing a learning group it is important to explain at an early stage the nature of your own agenda if you have one. You might have a number of aims, for example:

- To work on a collective research project.
- To set up a small-scale newsletter.
- To collaborate on an article for a journal or newspaper.
- To share learning resources such as reading lists.

If you can make clear your intentions and expectations then it will be easier to establish relationships with people. As others join your group for the agreed purpose, it may be necessary from time to time to redefine the goals, as they may become diffuse as time passes.

Groups tend to be held together by a sense of shared purpose, and it is important to keep redefining this. Learning groups may be quite formal such as when a group develops into a committee which runs an organisation. On the other hand, groups may remain at a very informal level which is akin to simply being a network. This will be a loose organisation of people who contact each other from time to time when there is a specific purpose, but do not generally come together formally. Learning and studying are activities which tend to thrive on collaborative activity, and being a member of one or more groups, whether formal or informal, is an important way of sustaining the learning process. Gibbs (1994) contains useful strategies on teamwork in learning.

Summary

- Always keep an open mind about the chance of setting up contacts.
- If the opportunity presents itself, set up a learning group quickly by exchanging addresses.
- Make sure your group remains focused on its main purpose for being connected.

Learning by teaching others

Teaching is, without doubt, one of the best ways of learning. Many teachers I know support this idea. In order to be able to teach something well, you first need to sort out your own ideas about it clearly, and to be able to present the material in a logical, understandable way. There is also in the process of explaining something, a sense of putting our own ideas in order. The two go hand in hand.

It follows then, that as part of studying you should take every opportunity to 'teach'. This does not necessarily mean standing up in front of a class, for teaching can take many forms. You could, however, start actively seeking opportunities to explain your own knowledge and understanding. It is important with your peers, however, not to sound too patronising or to make it seem as if you are a self-pronounced expert. The kind of language you choose can help here. If one of your friends says that he or she has not understood a lecture, then that is your chance! You can say 'Well, it seems to me that what the lecturer is saying is … etc. I might be wrong, but that seems to be the main point.'

Another good opportunity is when someone in your class has missed a lecture and they ask you to collect handouts and perhaps ask if they can borrow your notes to copy up. You can offer in this situation to explain your notes to them over a cup of coffee. Provided you do not go on too long, they will probably appreciate this help. You might also need them to reciprocate at some time.

Practical skills offer a golden opportunity for teaching your peers. There are so many areas where peer tutoring can be an enormous help. These might include:

- computer skills
- using a complex photocopier
- using the library catalogue system
- finding journal articles
- locating other learning resources (e.g. videos).

There are often many opportunities in large colleges and universities to help other students who may, for example, be visually-impaired or hearing-impaired. Such students are usually delighted to receive help with, say, having books read to them, or perhaps having someone explain in their own words what a lecturer has said. Providing learning support for your peers not only helps them, but enables you to learn by teaching.

If you have been learning something and have not quite mastered it, then the following strategy may help. Try writing a short tuition guide to the topic as if you were writing it for one of your peers. Set down the key concepts in a logical order, and explain briefly and clearly the main ideas of the subject. When complete, hand it to a friend and ask them to go through it marking in red every time an instruction or explanation was not clear. You can then study the subject further and try to improve your guide. The very process of writing your short guide will probably help you to understand the topic yourself.

You can practise your teaching skills in a number of ways. Those of you with children will know how demanding it is to explain a fairly complex idea to a child when they ask you to explain something to them. It is very difficult to do this in simple language while still retaining the essence of the truth of the idea. Another practical strategy is to take a relatively simple idea such a rewiring a three-pin electric plug, and try to write a clear set of instructions on what to do and what safety precautions to observe. Try to set down your instructions in clear, unambiguous and succinct language. Then hand your instructions to someone else to follow, or try to follow them yourself, strictly carrying out to the letter what you are asked to do. You will soon find out if you have written clear instructions.

Summary

- Practise teaching; it is one of the best ways of learning.
- Reciprocal peer teaching is an excellent study strategy.
- Look for ways of helping fellow students who may have a learning disability which limits their capacity to study.

Being a mentor

A mentor is a person who takes a personal interest in your academic and professional development, and by providing support, advice and encouragement, assists you to progress in your chosen field. A mentor may be someone in your place of work, or where you study, or simply someone you know. It is implicit in the philosophy of mentoring that the mentor has greater knowledge and experience of the subject of the mentoring relationship than the mentee (person being mentored). However, someone who is a mentee in one relationship may be a mentor to another person.

Perhaps the closest established relationship to that of mentor, is the role of research supervisor to a research student working on a doctorate. The supervisor helps the student with the design of the research and the structure of the thesis, but also offers general help and encouragement.

The role of mentor is becoming recognised as very helpful in the workplace. It is particularly helpful when someone is appointed to a new job or gains a promotion. The mentor will act as a guide and reference point for the newcomer, helping them with difficulties as they arise. Some organisations officially appoint mentors, in order to ensure that all staff have the benefit of someone to turn to. If this is the case, employees are often given the chance to request that a particular person be their mentor.

Unless you find yourself part of an official mentoring system, then you may either wish to help someone by being their mentor, or seek a mentor for yourself. Of course, mentoring relationships do not normally arise because you go up to a person and ask them to be your mentor! You would probably start by asking someone who appeared to be knowledgeable in your area, if perhaps they could recommend any relevant literature, and if they could tell you about their own studies. If the relationship was going to develop into a mentoring relationship, then it would happen slowly, and gradually evolve as both mentor and mentee develop confidence in each other. Mentoring relationships do not need to last forever. They can grow, last while they are useful, and then gradually fade away. It is important that in a mentoring relationship, neither mentor nor mentee wishes to take or gain too much from the relationship. The mentee clearly is looking for help and advice, but will also contribute to the mentor in terms of providing feedback on the effectiveness of the advice. The mentor on the other hand should not in any way exploit the implicit position of power which they hold. The mentor should be motivated purely by the desire to help and guide and offer their own experience and knowledge for the help of others.

The mentor relationship should always be a voluntaristic one. The relationship implies that either the mentor or the mentee can withdraw at any time if the relationship develops in a way which is felt to be unacceptable. The mentor may find that the relationship is too time-consuming for example; while the mentee may find that the mentor starts to impose his or her views rather too much.

As people will have helped you with your studies, it is natural as you develop your own knowledge and expertise, that you should wish to help others where you can. You may be approached by someone who recognises your knowledge, or you may offer to help someone in a small way. It is important that such offers of help should be on a fairly limited scale at first in order to allow the relationship to develop gradually. Large-scale offers of assistance may be rather overwhelming for the mentee, and create too much dependence.

Many relationships are in fact that of mentor/mentee without being accorded that specific name. The participants may never think of themselves as being a mentor or a mentee. As you develop in terms of studying it is very rewarding to think that you can contribute in terms of passing on study skills and knowledge to others. You are then part of the endless process of the transmission of knowledge and culture from one generation to another. Knowledge must be transmitted or it would gradually cease to be known. Not only is there a transmission of knowledge longitudinally from one person to another and to another, but there is also a cyclical transmission of knowledge. The mentor helps the mentee, who in turn through feedback, gives the mentor a fresh view of the world. Studying, learning from others, and then passing on that teaching is one of the most fundamental and exciting of all human activities.

Summary

- Both mentor and mentee help and inform each other through the mentoring process.
- The mentoring relationship should be one of freedom, where either participant can continue or withdraw from the relationship as they consider appropriate.

REFERENCES AND BIBLIOGRAPHY

Audi, R. (1995) *The Cambridge Dictionary of Philosophy*. Cambridge, Cambridge University Press.

Bullock, A. and Stallybrass, O. (1977) *The Fontana Dictionary of Modern Thought*. London, Fontana.

Buzan, T. (1988) *Make the Most of Your Mind*. London, Pan Books.

Buzan, T. (1989) *Use Your Head*. London, BBC Books.

Church, J. (1997) *Social Trends*. London, The Stationery Office.

Cook, C. (ed.) (1994) *Pears Cyclopaedia*. London, Penguin.

Crystal, D. (1994) *The Cambridge Concise Encyclopedia*. Cambridge, Cambridge University Press.

Dennis, G. (1995) *Annual Abstract of Statistics*. London, HMSO.

Fowler, H.W. (1968) *A Dictionary of Modern English Usage*. Oxford, Oxford University Press.

Gibbs, G. (1994) *Learning in Teams: A Student Manual*. Oxford, Oxford Centre for Staff Development.

Goldsmith, E. and Hildyard, N. (1992) *The Earth Report 3: An A–Z Guide to Environmental Issues*. London, Mitchell Beazley.

Heap, B. (1997) *The Complete Degree Course Offers*. Richmond, Trotman.

Howard, G. (1994) *The Good English Guide*. London, Macmillan.

Hudson, R. et al. (eds) (1997) *Flexible Learning in Action*. London, Kogan Page.

Jaques, D. (1991) *Learning in Groups*. London, Kogan Page.

Jones, B. and Johnson, R. (1990) *Making the Grade, Vol. 1: Reading and Learning*. Manchester, Manchester University Press.

Jones, B. and Johnson, R. (1990) *Making the Grade, Vol. 2: Thinking and Writing*. Manchester, Manchester University Press.

Lloyd, S.M. (1982) *Roget's Thesaurus of English Words and Phrases*. Harlow, Longman.

McGivney, V. (1996) *Staying or Leaving the Course: Non-completion and Retention of Mature Students in Further and Higher Education*. Leicester, NIACE.

Rees, N. (1994) *Brewer's Quotations: a Phrase and Fable Dictionary*. London, Cassell.

The Stationery Office (1998) *Whitaker's Almanack*. London, The Stationery Office.

Vacher Dod Publishing (1997) *The Vacher Dod Guide to the New House of Commons 1997*. London, Vacher Dod.

Whitear, G. (1995) *The NVQ and GNVQ Handbook*. London, Pitman.

INDEX

TEACH YOURSELF

WRITING ESSAYS & REPORTS

Paul Oliver

The daunting blank page, the chewed-up pen, the cold sweat – when the pressure's on, what should you do to meet your deadline with a brilliant and well-polished essay?

Teach Yourself Writing Essays & Reports is the book for all students that will help you write first class assignments at college and university. An experienced university tutor, Paul Oliver tells you about the conventions that will help you structure your ideas into essays, seminar papers, research studies, reports and portfolios. He shows you how to avoid plagiarism and jargon, how to write an introduction and a conclusion, and how to construct a bibliography. There is a section on editing, and advice on how to get help from your own tutor.

Other related titles

TEACH YOURSELF

RESEARCH

Paul Oliver

Teach Yourself Research describes the nature of the research process from the initial design of an investigation, through the process of data collection and analysis, to the writing of the final research report. It emphasises that research methods can be used in a wide variety of jobs and situations, and that it is not difficult to carry out straightforward research which can yield valuable results. The book encourages the reader to plan and take part in practical enquiries.

The book:

- takes the reader through the entire research process from initial design to presenting results;
- uses examples of research from business, industry, education and everyday life;
- stresses the practical uses of research, and in particular for developing organisational policy;
- meets the needs of college and university students who are studying research methods; professional people who collect and analyse data in their jobs; and those who wish to use research methods to help them pursue a personal interest more seriously.

The author is a university lecturer who teaches research methods at higher degree level and also supervises research students. He is interested in seeing research methods understood and used more widely, and is also the author of *Writing Essays and Reports* in the Teach Yourself series.